CW01371189

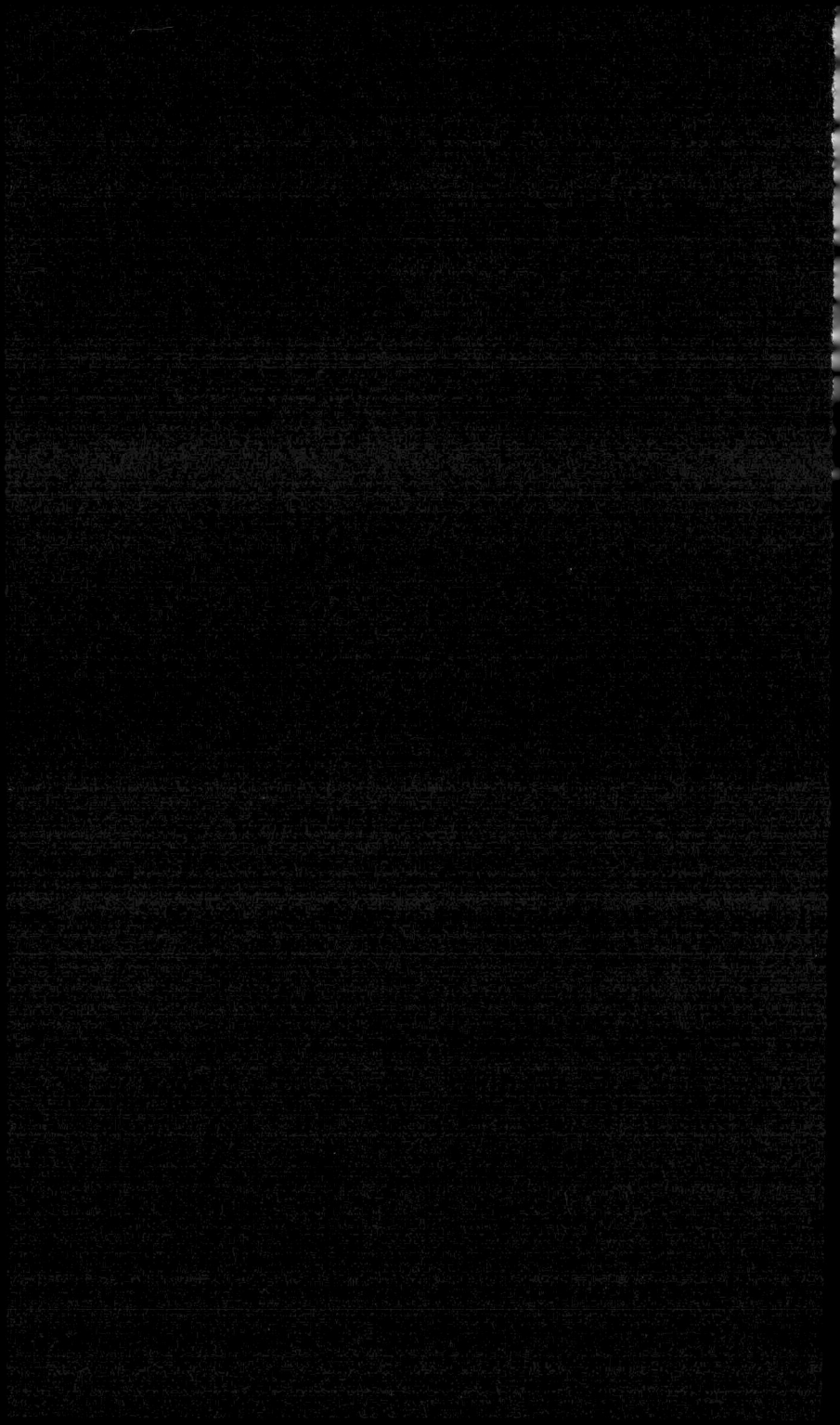

THE ALCHEMY LECTURE SERIES

The annual Alchemy Lecture is a collaboration between York University and Knopf Canada. Grounded in the idea of alchemy as a "form of speculative thought" and "a process of transformation and creation," it brings together distinguished thinkers from different disciplines and geographies to address the most pressing issues of our times. Each year, the Lecture takes the form of a live, multi-vocal public event presented by York University followed by a book published under the Alchemy imprimatur at Knopf Canada.

PREVIOUS LECTURES
Borders, Human Itineraries, and All Our Relation

THE ALCHEMY LECTURE

Five Manifestos for the
Beautiful World

THE ALCHEMY LECTURE

Five Manifestos for the Beautiful World

PHOEBE BOSWELL
SAIDIYA HARTMAN
JANAÍNA OLIVEIRA
JOSEPH M. PIERCE
CRISTINA RIVERA GARZA

Introduction by
CHRISTINA SHARPE

ALCHEMY
BY KNOPF CANADA

Copyright © 2024 Phoebe Boswell, Saidiya Hartman,
Janaína Oliveira, Joseph M. Pierce and Cristina Rivera Garza
Introduction copyright © 2024 Christina Sharpe

All rights reserved under International and Pan-American Copyright Conventions. No part of this book may be reproduced in any form or by any electronic or mechanical means, including information storage and retrieval systems, without permission in writing from the publisher, except by a reviewer, who may quote brief passages in a review. Published in 2024 by Alchemy by Knopf Canada, a line of books within Alfred A. Knopf Canada, a division of Penguin Random House Canada Limited, Toronto. Distributed in Canada and the United States of America by Penguin Random House Canada Limited, Toronto.

www.penguinrandomhouse.ca

Alchemy by Knopf Canada and colophon are registered trademarks.

Library and Archives Canada Cataloguing in Publication

Title: Five manifestos for the beautiful world / Phoebe Boswell, Saidiya Hartman, Janaína Oliveira, Joseph M. Pierce, Cristina Rivera Garza ; editor, Christina Sharpe.
Names: Boswell, Phoebe, 1982- author. | Hartman, Saidiya V., author. | Oliveira, Janaina, author. | Pierce, Joseph M., author. | Rivera Garza, Cristina, 1964- author. | Sharpe, Christina Elizabeth, editor.
Description: Series statement: Alchemy lecture | Second Alchemy Lecture held at York University, Toronto, on November 2, 2023. | Includes bibliographical references.
Identifiers: Canadiana (print) 20240310454 | Canadiana (ebook) 20240310543 | ISBN 9781039055971 (hardcover) | ISBN 9781039055988 (EPUB)
Subjects: LCSH: Aesthetics.
Classification: LCC BH211 .F58 2024 | DDC 111/.85—dc23

Text design: Jennifer Griffiths
Jacket design: Jennifer Griffiths
Typeset by: Terra Page

Printed in Canada

10 9 8 7 6 5 4 3 2 1

ALCHEMY
BY KNOPF CANADA

Penguin
Random House
Canada

CONTENTS

Introduction by Christina Sharpe 1

"A Manifesto for Speculative Relations"
JOSEPH M. PIERCE
7

"A Manifesto for Curation"
JANAÍNA OLIVEIRA
39

"Manifesto of the As Yet Unlived Thing"
PHOEBE BOSWELL
63

"Crow Jane Makes a Modest Proposal"
SAIDIYA HARTMAN
97

"Subjunctive: A Manifesto About Language, Territory, and the Yet to Come"
CRISTINA RIVERA GARZA
117

Notes and References 153
About the Alchemists 164
Acknowledgements 167

INTRODUCTION

The Alchemy Lecture is interested in producing new modes of apprehending and changing the conditions of our contemporary world. The enduring principle is that, in times like these, of great crises—climate catastrophe, human catastrophe (the weaponizing and hardening of borders, the planned re-invasion of Haiti by another name, continued occupation, settler colonialism, forced movement and immiseration of people all over the world, genocides in Sudan, the Democratic Republic of Congo, and Gaza Jenin Rafah)—we must resist the siloing of people and think/make/do. And we must risk something toward bringing into being other ways of living together.

Last year's inaugural Alchemy Lecture was "Borders, Human Itineraries, and all our Relation." I want to bring forward a few of the questions and a charge that animated it: first, "What environments must we foster to imagine the world anew after the undoing?" (Adeyemo); and second, "What is the language we need to live right now? . . . I mean the language of words, speech, and text. What should we talk about when so many words exist to destroy us?" (Diaz). The charge was that we engage in the work of the "ongoing invention of new languages of the collective" (Walcott).

"Five Manifestos for the Beautiful World" goes some way toward answering those questions, posing new ones, and working in the materials of that charge.

A manifesto is a public declaration, a written statement declaring publicly the intentions, motives, or views of its issuer. A manifesto starts in the condition that we are enduring and ruminates on the dire circumstances and perhaps the illusions that we inhabit. A manifesto is a critique and an urgent call to action that often contains a resolve *to* action. That resolve might be to gathering; it might be to dreaming. Gathering, speaking, dreaming, and writing are each powerful actions in the face of structural violence, genocide, and repression.

What must be made manifest, confronted, spoken in these catastrophic times includes the rejection of that which is manufactured as consent and the offering in its place of another set of understandings and imaginings of the given world and the made world. As Rinaldo Walcott reminds us, the struggle for and over meaning is real.

These Alchemy Lectures make clear that a lecture is not a spectacle: it is a gathering; it is a communion; we meet, here, to make plans, to see a way—many ways—to go on.

Each of these manifestos speaks from the structural conditions under which we live and labor, in order to address the crises that we are living through.

Relation is an invitation to live. **Joseph M. Pierce** (Cherokee Nation) offers a "manifesto as storying," "a manifesto for multiplicity, for the vibrational possibilities of kinship," an invitation to join the work involved in the making and sustaining of relation and our mutual thriving. He ends in dancing.

There are urgencies that move us to the work of care. **Janaína Oliveira** (Brazil) begins in the "dance dancing;" she then proceeds to elaborate a collective exercise of care as curation where curation ("care, cultivation, healing") for a beautiful world strives to "reconstruct . . . imaginaries, so that death, violence, and oblivion are not automatically identified as places of belonging."

There is an architecture to replace those militaristic and brutal imaginations. **Phoebe Boswell** (UK/Kenya) begins in 2020 with the terrors of COVID-19 and moves us through the failed imaginations of politicians and art-world establishments to a proposition: what, "if we're lucky and brave," might then be the work of the artist—to "make our own little worlds within our work [where] we invite people in and hope that these worlds might somehow ignite something that moves us towards the belief in a new place."

The kinds of violences enacted on Black life that are sometimes embraced as possibility must be abandoned; **Saidiya Hartman** (US) gives us a polemic and a satire that lays bare and skewers the brutal neoliberal logics that produce what the comedian Ryan Ken so aptly called "diversity and inclusion war crimes" and what Saidiya names "the gift of pragmatism[:] a profound tolerance of the unlivable."

INTRODUCTION

The subjunctive is a tense for living and **Cristina Rivera Garza** (Mexico/US) offers us fifteen theses where it is such a grammar: "If we were to write a house. If a house were a communal pact, a collaborative belaboring, a form of direct action that required the time of others, their hands and lungs, their eyes, their hope. If a house were the opposite of war." And in the final thesis: "In the subjunctive, no one takes anyone's life."

Words matter. As Toni Cade Bambara tells us, "Words are to be taken seriously. I try to take seriously acts of language. Words set things in motion. I've seen them doing it. Words set up atmospheres, electrical fields, charges. I've felt them doing it. Words conjure. I try not to be careless about what I utter, write, sing. I'm careful about what I give voice to."[1]

The powerful address uncertainty with brutality; the powerful address dissent with brutality; the powerful address most everything with brutality. These five manifestos contend that the Beautiful World is not a touristic world of consumption and extraction, but one that meets Dionne Brand's understanding of beauty, that it is "not uncomplicated . . . Beauty is the ability to see everything; to confront everything."[2] How must we live? What architecture might facilitate that living? What urgencies move us? What delusions of inclusion are long past time to abandon? What is the tense of our speaking, the tense of our doing?

That we gather in this time of catastrophe, matters. That we speak in this time of catastrophe, matters. I am grateful to gather here with intention, to read the words of these five Alchemists and their manifestos for the Beautiful World.

—CHRISTINA SHARPE, Toronto, 2024

CRISTINA RIVERA GARZA

The subjunctive is the smuggler who crosses the border of the future bearing unknown cargo.

If we knew the word for *relative* in every Indigenous
language, then what futures would we hold dear?

JOSEPH M. PIERCE

A Manifesto for Speculative Relations

JOSEPH M. PIERCE

A Tessellating Reverberation

On this September night, I am undone by the beating heart of a people. We stomp a ground that has known generations of our songs of hope and renewal, our memories and lamentations. Ancient cadences coax the gathered to life. Women mark time with rock-filled turtle shells bound to their ankles by leather cords, giving shape to the insistence of our bodies in relation.

I have lost myself in the warmth of belonging. We trace circles around a breathing fire. As our luscious bodies groove this earth, we are released from gravity's clutches, unencumbered by reality, spiraling.

I often want to escape reality. But forgetting is a dangerous business. We are not afforded such oblivion, we who bear the blood memory of removal to this place that was not ours, but which we have made home. This is a land of different rivers, different winds, but one whose whispers have become familiar. I'd like to forget that there were settlers laughing while Cherokee people were rounded up in concentration camps, marched at gunpoint, and forced to walk the Trail of Tears.[1] We were sent to a place called Indian Territory, not knowing how to behold its subtle curves. Not knowing how to sing its songs. I'd like to forget that cosmic rupture.

This land is not where fire was first given to us by tiny Water Spider, but we carried an ember of that unending flame (even when everything else was taken) and reignited it here, a glimmer lingering from ancestral time. This smoldering finds a way to burn inside of me, a summoning of light on bodies that hum in tessellating reverberation.

What does it take to remember bodies lost to time?

What does it take to dance the fire to life?

There are answers to these questions. But they take the shape of a river, a stomp dance, a basket, a story. They taste like stardust, these answers of carbon and sweetgrass. They form in the becoming-multiple that we conjure from the depths of a tale about how the world was made, how fire was gifted to the people, how a constellation came to exist in the night sky.

Stories teach us how to act, how to love, how to relate. They fill our worlds with possibility; they remind us of what we have lost. Stories burn in our hearts, remnants of our own bodies, traces of past lives brought to bear on the present, leaning into the future.

I think of this manifesto as storying—an enactment of the heliacal rising of smoke from a fire that knows no boundaries, only the elegance of time folding back on itself. This work resists colonial hungers, those devouring appetites that settlers call capital, empire, property, man. I dwell on stories because through them we learn to place ourselves in relation to spirits, land, and kin. By dwelling on the articulation of story as relation—to relate is also to story—this is a manifesto for multiplicity, for the vibrational possibilities of kinship. It is an attempt to transmit desire and love and rage—all at once, burning—across these pages, to your hands, to your heart. It is to behold the glint of a rebellious star, to smile a knowing smile—an attempt at conjuring life from the archives of Indigenous disappearance, and in so doing, realize that the ancestors, the fire, have been there all along.

This is a manifesto for speculative relations.

Guiding Light

Let me share the story of the Pleiades and the Pine Tree, as the guiding light for this invitation to relate:

There is a boy who does not like to do his chores. Instead of helping his mother, every chance he gets he runs outside to dance. And not just any dance—the stomp dance that is supposed to be performed only on certain occasions. But he loves dancing so much, he just can't help himself. And his joy is contagious. He convinces his six brothers to join him instead of doing their chores, too. This goes on for months. Their mother gets so frustrated that one day, she decides she'll teach them all a lesson. She puts rocks in their porridge at dinner time. The unsuspecting boys crunch down on the rocks and scream with pain. Thinking she has got through to them, their mother says: "That's what you get for not helping me!" The boys are embarrassed, angry, so angry that they run outside and start to dance. Around and around they go, spiraling. They begin to rise into the air. Their mother goes looking for them and is terrified by what she sees. Her boys are floating in the sky! She jumps as high as she can and grabs one of her son's legs. She pulls him down, and he strikes the ground with such force that he is swallowed up by the earth. The remaining six boys rise to the heavens and become the Pleiades constellation. Their mother is despondent at the loss of her boys. She cries in the spot where her son had been swallowed by the earth, and from her tears, a pine tree grows, reaching up toward the heavens.[2]

Some boys become stars. Some become trees. Some boys just want to dance. These transformations teach us how the heavens hold our ancestors, our kin, living reminders of our stories and of our commitments to each other. The Pleiades and the Pine are related, tied to each other through bonds of kinship. In this way, we understand that the middle world (Elohi) is related to both the upper world (Galvladi) and the under world (Elati or Elohi Hawinadidla). We understand our place in the cosmos as neither its center, nor its margins, but as part of an interconnected set of relationships that emerge across time and space. We are related to the stars and the trees. This is not metaphor. This is not myth.

There are thousands of similar stories from thousands of different Indigenous communities that teach of our relationships and responsibilities toward other beings. This is just one example. But I am using it as a touchstone because it hinges on celestial observation, on speculation, and on how kinship reaches across the heavens and earth.

This is a story about speculative relations. Like all stories, it is open to interpretation. Some may see a lesson in heeding one's mother—the boys are punished for not doing their chores. Others may think it is about how some people have a drive that leads them to do things out of order—dancing when they are not supposed to, an implacable impulse to find joy in spite of the drudgery of daily life. Or perhaps it is a story that asks us to imagine what possibilities are manifest when we listen to our hearts and to the rhythms that move us.

I love this story because it teaches us not just to look up at the stars, but *why* we look, and *what* that looking is meant to ask of us. When we look up at the Pleiades constellation, what Cherokee people call Ani Jogon, we are reminded of the boys who dance. They are still up there dancing, glimmering with movement. And we recall their brother, the Pine, who sways in the wind, growing strong and tall, wanting to join his brothers. In the wake of the pathway to the stars that these boys create, we are left wondering what kinds of futures we could have if we only paid attention to our fullness, to the insistence of our dreams for tomorrow.

These dreams for tomorrow are what I want to story here. I want to explode with these sidereal, irrepressible stories.

This one is the guiding light, the one that reminds me why I am writing, and more importantly, why I think others should listen. Embedded within this relation are more than just lessons about how to treat people; there are also lessons about how to search beyond, how to reach across the breach of time and find outside of yourself a point of contact, a tether to another world.

Two Clarifications

I have called this text a manifesto for speculative relations, so before we continue, allow me to explain these terms. *Speculation* comes from the Ancient Greek root *skop*, which was translated (and rearranged) to the late Latin root *spec*, thus *speculātiōn*, which was rendered in Old French as *speculacïon*, and in Old English as *speculacioun*.[3] Our contemporary usage still retains the Latin duality between a *speculum* (a mirror or other reflective surface) and *specula* (a watchtower or lookout). Thus, speculation is both to look *inward* in self-reflection, and to look *outward* in observation of the world beyond. When we look within, reflecting on what we have experienced, that speculation allows us to consider how our actions transform who we are. Likewise, when we look outside of ourselves, gazing at the horizon, the heavens, the stars, speculation is a method of considering the world from an embodied location, and thus from the perspective of our individual selves in relation.[4] In short, speculation refers to both sight and insight, and it is this dual meaning that I want to harness by imagining speculative relations.

By *relations* I mean the practices developed by Indigenous Peoples over millennia for engaging with human and other-than-human beings in ways that prioritize mutual respect, humility, and balance. Relations—and by extension, living in good relations—means upholding obligations of kinship in an ongoing way, committing to the responsibilities and practices of care that sustain community life, and enacting reciprocal recognition of human and other-than-human beings.[5] There are more and less complex ways of saying this, but the crucial point is that relations are a shorthand for the fullness of how we practice Indigeneity. Relations are not a singular act, nor are they universal practices. Each community has its own understanding of what it means to relate, to be a relative, to act in good relations. And each community has a sense of how the individual interacts with these collective understandings and responsibilities.

But a relation is also a story, an act of narration. If we put these understandings together as *speculative relations*, I am suggesting a creative practice that is grounded in ethical engagement with the land, humans, and other-than-human beings, and which also opens possibilities for storying ourselves and our communities into the future. I am recalling that Indigenous relational paradigms should be understood as at once singular and collective, past- and future-oriented, a balance between ancestral practices and open-ended possibilities. Our relations are land-based, but they are also speculative. By attending to the speculative aspects of relations, and by relating in speculative ways, we can better support decolonial practices.

A final clarification: I cannot speak on behalf of all Indigenous people (lol), the Cherokee Nation, or even my own kin. I can offer my thoughts on what the concept of relations has meant to me and could mean to others. This position is grounded in my own cultural background. Cherokee governance was traditionally non-coercive, a set of continually renewed agreements that could be refused if an individual or group felt the need to do so.[6] Cherokee storytelling, likewise, did not pontificate, but asked each listener to hone their skills of interpretation and act in accordance with the lessons learned, lessons that would evolve over the span of one's life.[7] You may refuse, walk away from, or ignore what I say; you may take these thoughts and mold them to your own lived experience; you may revisit this and draw new conclusions later. It is not my place to tell you, or anyone, what to do. But it is my intention to share what futures might be possible if we relate, if we speculate together, dreaming otherwise futures to life.[8]

The Argument

LAND

The logical extension of decolonization in the Americas is the return of all land to those from whom it was stolen.[9] The call is simple: #LandBack. That is what decolonization means. The problem is not the argument. The problem is its materiality. The land. The water. The life.

The argument is only a problem if we start from a premise that requires it be justified as an expression of Western logic, a logic that would in turn require a justification of the very life that the argument aims to save. I refuse to justify human and other-than-human life. I refuse to entertain the problem of why the land should be returned. Instead, I begin with the centrality of relations—of living and loving and insisting on the aliveness of our relational speculations. In other words, though the physical manifestation of the "problem" is the mattering of life itself, we cannot begin to approach this question, this land, from the perspective of colonial modernity. We must start with the land as the matrix, the framework, and the dynamic, expansive, presence of life lived in good relations.

Land is territory: the air, water, sub-, super-, and terranean life that exists irrespective of human presence, but which engages with humans as part of a millenarian tradition—an ancestral relationality that flourishes through respectful and reciprocal engagement over time. Land is a shorthand for the territorial expansiveness that Indigenous Peoples seek to restore through decolonization, and to maintain through living in good relations.

Land is not a scale of taxonomically ordered objects. We admit no hierarchies here. Land is neither property, capital, nor simply place. We refuse the logics of capitalist alienation and accumulation. We refuse land as a regime of property. Land is not something that can be owned or acquired. It is the network of relationships that place supports, vibrant and tectonic, an unending, expansive imbrication. Land is the tensile connection between beings who relate, becoming multiple in the expression of their intimate, enduring connections. Land is the inter-oscillating hum of beings in relation.

It is not hard to make the ethical leap from "you stole the land" to "you must give it back." But settlers are stubborn. I can hear them asking: Give it back how? Give it back to whom? I do not know how to solve the question of *how*. I don't think anyone does. What I do know is that *how* is not something that the existing colonial paradigm is equipped to carry out.

But let us be honest: We are still living in a colonial society in which the structural conditions for life are predicated on the hierarchical ordering of bodies and knowledges. This ongoing colonial project renders unthinkable, unlivable, any deviation from the Western conception of man (what Sylvia Wynter calls the overrepresented Man, or Man 1).[10] This ongoing colonial project, its architecture and infrastructure, its framing of knowledge and power as the exclusive domain of whiteness, of men, of modernity, is what Christina Sharpe calls "the weather," and "the totality of the environments in which we struggle; the machines in which we live."[11] Ongoing colonial modernity means that the only way to make life livable for all is to find new ways (or return to old ways) of understanding the possibilities of life. Life, and by extension land, cannot be thought through from within the colonial paradigm that objectified, propertied, and destroyed it. A decolonial approach to land must be thought otherwise.

Eve Tuck and K. Wayne Yang remind us not only that decolonization is not a metaphor, but also that "decolonization specifically requires the repatriation of Indigenous land and life."[12] Returning lifeways requires that Indigenous people be able to flourish. Our flourishing is non-negotiable. Our flourishing is part and parcel with the return of land because the land is not returned to us under the regime of property, but in relation to us as part of the interlocking web of kinship that makes life possible in the first place. Indigenous land co-constitutes Indigenous life.

"Give it back" names only part of the issue. What is more, as we have discussed, land is not an "it," but a network, reaching back into ancestral time and pushing us toward the future. Land cannot be contained by the grammars of Western knowledge. Land exists. Land dreams. Land endures. Land only requires that we give it back to itself. Let me try this sentence again without the alienating thingification: Land only requires landing. Land only asks for freedom, for land as land. Land only wants us to land and be landed in return.

We have to reframe the issue. For this decolonial future to become possible, the guiding force must no longer be capital but relations.

RELATIONS

The primary goal of colonization is the destruction of Indigenous relations. The destruction is not simply of Indigenous people, the theft not simply of land and bodies but of the possibility of enacting the relations that make us human. Opaskwayak Cree scholar Shawn Wilson puts this elegantly: "Rather than viewing ourselves as being *in* relationship with other people or things, we *are* the relationships that we hold and are part of."[13] I am not simply an individual with relationships. I am constituted by the relationships that sustain me. My being is never singular, never isolated. I am never a discrete individual. *I am* is a phrase that always requires an understanding of being-in-relation. *I am* implies multiplicity; and the enactment of relations renders that individual whole through an expansive manifestation of belonging.

Relations allow us to undertake the real task of coming to terms with our battered selves, poisoned water, land on the brink of ruination. Relations are the abiding principles by which our futures can be imagined anew. Relations are not a metaphor, but the enactment of reciprocity in our everyday occupations, spiritual engagements, and conceptual projections.

But here is the challenging part. Though decolonization is material, it is also an act of faith, a process by which the methods of engaging with reciprocity and accountability, the solemn practice of living in good relations, are enacted. It is material in the sense that it deals with the physicality of our world, but because this world is understood by Indigenous Peoples to be populated not by inert objects ("matter") but rather by animate and life-giving relatives (beings), this materiality must be equally thought of as an epistemic and ontological arrangement by which the vibrancy of life, in its unimaginable diversity, is returned to itself. Thus, the question of how to return the land to this or that people is less important (in my view) than restoring the ethical imperatives of reciprocity and relationality that sustain all life on this planet.

This is not hyperbole. For the earth to survive, the predominance of European, capitalist modernity, its settler colonial and imperialist structures, extractive economies, binary gendering, racializing taxonomies, epistemological impoverishment, and unending thirst for "resources," must end. This is what Maya Quiché scholar Emil' Keme means when he says, "for Abiayala to live, the Americas must die."[14] Using the Guna people's term, Abiayala, for the land in its full maturity, Keme invites us to reject the conceptual framing of the "American" continent as a whole. He calls for us to let go of the structures that have built the concept of *America* (both "North America" and "Latin America"), which was only ever an invention of settler governments and avaricious conquistadors. Only ever—but these ideas are deeply ingrained. Settler maps call this land America, prioritizing nation-states and the names they gave to the territories they stole from Indigenous Peoples. Indigenous names have largely been erased from colonial maps by colonial governments in this colonial modernity. Such naming was meant to erase our territories and our relatives. But the land is there, landing; the relatives are there, relating.

Sometimes I try to find ways to say this, and words fail. Or they must be stretched to encompass more than what they seem to give. I think of words like *co-constitutive*, *mutuality*, *reciprocity*. I try to find a way to explain that our being is inherently multiple. That we are intercorporeal, intercosmical. These forms of describing our braiding, entwining subjectivities must be liberated from the isolating technologies of settler colonial domination. They, we, must demand our fullness. Our multiplicity.

The idea we must reject is that the human individual is the sole actor in the world, with everything else relegated to the category of object, inert and unfeeling. We must reject the facile move to center the human in our thinking and our actions. The trick is to find ways to describe what happens when the self is imbricated, enmeshed, with the ongoing vitality of others—other beings and spirits and things (that are not just things) that act in this world (and beyond). But we must do so without relying on the stereotype of the mystical Indian, without entering the domain of caricature. The trick is to find a way to describe our calling-into-being, which is irrevocably and undoubtedly the product of some set of forces outside of us, but which nevertheless communicates with us, if we listen, if we know how to observe, to speculate.

Let me put this differently: while the argument for decolonization does not admit deviation from the precept of land back, the return of land requires the capacity to speculate relations—that is, to consider the ways we are fully formed only ever in relation to other beings, and that in order to realize this relationality we must enact the dual meanings of speculation. We must consider our positions, our place, and the ethical imperatives that ground us, while also looking beyond the isolating individual and toward the possible, to what imminent becomings might present themselves on the horizon. We have to balance the space-time of being with the conceptual possibilities of dreams.

BALANCE

Relationality means extending yourself toward others in a humble, generous way, with gratitude and conviction, with the goodness of heart that characterizes the ethical system of communion and reciprocity with others. It means daring to be affected by what is outside yourself. Becoming porous. Becoming part of the ongoingness of creation, in its multiplicity and its transformations. It means refusing to accept the ontological limitations of Western science in favor of cosmological truths that defy positivist accounts of the real. It means living in the supposed unreality of our pluriversal politics while striving to expand the living truth of the world toward something more, something not yet realized, on the horizon, a speculation.

It took me a long time to have a sense of what it meant to think of myself as already part of an ongoing process of relationality with other beings. This is spiritual work. It sometimes means leaving behind academic training, and instead leaning on feeling, on the sense of the world as it manifests in you, through your pores, as it resonates in your bones. Not feeling as in "because I feel this way," but with an understanding of what it feels like to live in balance, in relation. For example, Cherokee elder Hastings Shade describes Cherokee ethics as an embodied, holistic relationship with the world. As fellow Cherokee Christopher B. Teuton explains, drawing on Shade's teachings, to navigate the world in a good way means "'standing in the middle,' a way of relating to the center or middle (ayetli) within ourselves and maintaining balance in the modern world through living in tohi [balance, peace, or flow] of body, mind, and spirit."[15] The connection between body, mind, and spirit is crucial. It is this sense that gives rise to centering, "to stand in the middle" (in Cherokee, "ayetli tsidoga"), to living a good life in balance with the forces of nature and the cosmos, and, I would add, allowing time for introspection, for speculating on the right way to approach a problem. One cannot stand in the middle without being in touch with the physical, intellectual, and spiritual dimensions of the universe as they are reflected in our engagements with people and situations that emerge. To achieve this balance, this tohi, which is more an ideal state than a constantly lived reality, we have to open our minds and hearts to the feelings and practices of solidarity, reciprocity, and mutuality that define our relational ethics. We have to be open to the possibilities of correcting course, being brought back into balance—which is to say, we have to constantly interrogate, in a holistic way, the ethical and spiritual dimensions of our actions.

An example: I remember teaching a graduate seminar a few years ago about queer theory. We were reading the Spanish philosopher Paul B. Preciado's 2008 book *Testo Junkie*, discussing how Preciado understands the role of biopolitics in determining the possibilities (and limitations) of gender. I had a realization in the middle of the lecture and blurted out: "He doesn't understand that the body is sacred." The word *sacred* took the air out of the room. Perhaps everyone would have agreed with "the body is discourse," "the body is performative," or "the body is gestural." But "the body is *sacred*" seemed antithetical to the drive of Western theorizations that consider the body only through its materiality, divorced from metaphysics or spirituality. "The body is sacred" seemed somehow blasphemous in a classroom dedicated to the study of . . . the body.

To be fair, Preciado was writing about the contemporary rise of the pharmaceutical industry and the effects of that industry on how we see, understand, and inhabit gender. His work is ultimately concerned with the way new (and old) technologies impact the body, what it means, what it can become. He is not interested in spirituality (which is fine). But the approach to the body, which for Preciado is primarily Foucauldian, demonstrates how the regimes of knowledge-power, of sexuality, of self—the archaeological approach to epistemology—have become so pervasive in the academy as to go unnoticed, unremarked. I don't have a problem with Preciado or Foucault so much as with the pervasiveness of a materialist critique that somehow renders the body a textual production rather than a breathing, fleshed, cosmic possibility. The body must be both flesh and evanescence, both weight and spirituality.

Thinking back on this moment, perhaps I did not have the words to explain why I suddenly became concerned with this lack, this divorce of the material of the body from the cosmic. I meant that while the structuring elements of contemporary Western society—like discourse and history—can describe the way our bodies are repeatedly constructed within a social context, those elements cannot account for the spiritual aspect of Indigenous ways of thinking and doing, specifically relating to forces beyond the individual, beyond the physical. I meant that the Western avant-garde of gender theory cannot incorporate (cannot fathom, really) the relational paradigms of Indigenous thought that necessarily include spiritual engagements with the land, ancestors, humans, and other-than-human beings. I meant that biopolitics is insufficient to contemplate the Indigenous body from within an Indigenous paradigm.

I want to clarify one thing here. I am not saying that the body is sacred in a Christian sense, and therefore predicated on a binary, heterosexual norm. Not that. I am also not saying that queer theory is "bad." I mean that there are certain aspects of queer theory (and post-structuralism generally), such as its lack of engagement with non-discursive, and in this case spiritual, elements, that have real, tangible effects on how Indigenous people understand ourselves in relation to the past, present, and future (time), and especially to the land (place). I am saying that the spiritual need not be partitioned off as part of a subset of additional elements to consider when discussing the body, but rather must be a foundational aspect of how the body becomes a body, and of how the individual is related to the various other beings and ideas and feelings and desires that populate our existence, that are our existence. In short, I am saying that we must contend with the relational paradigms of Indigenous epistemologies in order to fully appreciate what our bodies are, and what they are capable of becoming.

THE ARGUMENT, THEN

Decolonization means giving the land back so that Indigenous people can live in good relations, because our relations are how we express and maintain our peoplehood. Though colonization is structured as the theft of land, what that theft destroys is our relations, and in doing so, our ability to exist as human beings. Thus, the work of decolonization is the work of restoring our relations. But to do so, I am suggesting we must speculate on what that means and how that means today, and restore those relations so that we can be humans who live in good relations with the beings and bodies that populate our worlds. This is not a rhetorical exercise, but a call for living the plenitude of our relations. This call is not just to ask for land or to demand accountability from settlers, but to insist on the living, the enacting, of our relational selves, now and in the future.

If this argument is persuasive, then it is so not because of the discursive maneuvers requiring adherence to its precepts, but because the truth of the matter is simple: the land is our relative, and we are incomplete without it. If I have described the logic of the argument as simple, it is only because we tend to abstract notions like justice, humanity, and ethics, and in so doing, detach them from the material and spiritual realities of our bodies—our embodiment—in this world. But if this manifesto for speculative relations has asked something of you, I hope it is to see that to approach the possibilities of a more just future, we must—as Audre Lorde taught us—not look for the tools that built this still-colonial world, but instead look at once inward and toward the glimmering horizon beyond.

If/Then Statements for a Speculative Future

1. If colonization is an enterprise, then it is a thirst for death and debt. If settlers rely on a capitalist economy to prove their civilization, then that economy and that civilization must end, must be rendered a distant memory and a cautionary tale, if this world is to have a future. If modernity is that ideal, that architecture of capitalism, racism, and patriarchy that determines the futurity of all peoples, then modernity, too, must be rendered ash. It must, in this sense, become the prologue to a return to the relational, to those forms of breath that endure in us, as an extension of our bodies into the multiplicities of creation.

2. If decolonization is not a metaphor, then the work cannot be metaphorical.[16] If we are to undertake this non-metaphorical work, then our approach must also attend to the realities, the material effects, of Indigenous cosmologies—which necessarily include our spiritual lives, our ancestral relations, human and other-than-human kin. If our approach must include the spiritual and cosmological fullness of Indigenous life, then it must be at once relational and speculative; it must, in other words, not be predicated on the deterministic, positivist regime of settler knowledge, but expand beyond those limiting confines, toward the infinite, toward the possible.

3. If settler colonialism is a structure, not an event, then we cannot think in events but patterns, the flows of power across time and space.[17] If we are thinking about structures, then we cannot defer to History (at least canonical History) to interpret those structures for us, we who have always been its object of inquiry or else its footnote[18], but instead must theorize and historicize our own experiences, traumas, joys, our love, our bodies, so that History knows who we are. If History does not know us, or want to know us, on the terms we set out for ourselves, then History can go fuck itself. If History can go fuck itself, then a few other academic disciplines can, too: white queer theory, white feminism, Anthropology, English (except for y'all doing the work), Philosophy, and most of the social sciences.

If I have left something out here, then feel free to use the following space to recall other things that can fuck right off:

If these things can fuck off, then what do we do in the interim? If you have ideas, then feel free to write them down here:

4. If to live in good relations is the ethical imperative that guides my actions, then I cannot be the center of things. If I am not the center of things, then I must reach out, I must speculate, toward others, toward the possibilities of enacting good relations. If speculation is the mode of operation, and the enactment of good relations is the method, then being an Indigenous person, living, breathing as an Indigenous person, means that my responsibilities and engagements with the world must reflect the fullness of myself in all its complexity and density, myself as it is in relation to others. And if these others are not just human but more-than-human kin, the plants, animals, stars, stones, rivers, oceans, insects, spirits, memories, ancestors, then my relations are immanent and speculative. And if the speculation of my relations is a core part of being in good relations, because I cannot position my understanding of the world from the perspective of those other beings, then I must strive to enact the obligations, responsibilities, and faith that constitute our ongoing reciprocity.

5. If we knew the word for *relative* in every Indigenous language, then what futures would we hold dear? What forms of attachment, what longing, would we require of the world that has for so many years sought to destroy the land, the future? If we knew the contours of relationality, its undulating process, then perhaps we would stand a chance at living. If our lives and the filaments that attach us to each other, to the multi-layered worlds and multi-worlded universes and beyond, if those attachments which are our lives, which are the substance of our worldings, are mutually constitutive, then there can be no life without relation, there can be no sense of reason or balance or joy without the reciprocal engagement, the humility and the love, that make life livable. If life is to be livable, if it is to be an incessant drive not to destroy but to bring to full flowering the possibilities of our mutual thriving, which is to say, our becoming multiple in relation and in possibility, then the livable life must begin from the perspective not of a singular self, but of a holy speculation. If this livable life is to endure, to persist, then it must find new language, new gestures, new ceremonies to bring that life into existence.

6. If the possibilities of Indigenous life are predicated on living the fullness of our relations, and if those relations are sacred, then the sacredness of relations is what Indigenous futures are built with. If that building is a process that can only be carried out with a good heart, in balance (tohi), living in good relations, then the reactive, blistering critiques of white fuckery, while satisfying, are not in the end what will bring balance to the cosmos. We seek the good path. But if that fuckery, in all its manifestations, persists, despite our critiques, despite our pleas and remonstrations, despite our well-crafted arguments and our calls to dismantle the systems of oppression that constitute and sustain the fuckery, then we always have refusal. The refusal, as Audra Simpson has shown, leads to alternative pathways, to distinct, grounded possibilities for living as Indigenous people in this world. Which is to say, when we run out of fucks to give, we must remember refusal.

7. If this manifesto is to mean anything, it must not be that Indigenous people are human. We cannot begin or end there. If it is to mean anything, then it means our humanity is an expression of relations, the relations that buoy and sustain our practices of Indigeneity that have endured, even if lost to time and violence, even if sedimented, underground, and archaic, even if displayed in vitrines for tourists to gawk at. If our relations are an expression of our humanity, are what makes us human—knowing full well that our humanness is not the center of things—then this manifesto is an invitation not to humanize ourselves, but to relate.

8. If I filled this eight-thousand-word manifesto with the phrase "Land Back" over and over, it would repeat four thousand times. By my calculations, this would occupy about thirty printed pages and take about an hour to read. If this were a durational performance and I made an audience listen to me read "Land Back" for an hour, dropping each page on the floor like a fallen leaf, a blistering reminder of our presence, I wonder how many people would hear:

> Land Back. Land Back. Land Back. Land Back. Land Back. Land Back. Land Back. Land Back. Land Back. Land Back. Land Back. Land Back. Land Back. Land Back.
> Free Palestine. Free Palestine. Free Palestine. Free Palestine. Free Palestine. Free Palestine. Free Palestine.

On average, the internet tells me, one tree can produce 8,333 pages of virgin pulp paper printed single-sided. If we assume that the print run of this volume is five thousand copies, then it would take nine trees to print my thirty-page manifesto for the entire run. How many trees is this manifesto worth? Should I plant ten trees? The one extra tree leaving this world more oxygenated than before? Can that be the manifesto? Have we talked about praxis yet?

9. If the manifestation of our futures is the goal of this text, that is only because we have always been bringing them to life through our mutual imbrication—what anthropologists call kinship, but what we call living—that is the enactment of belonging. This belonging—to be part of something outside oneself—is the fact of our material reality that settlers have always sought to destroy. And it is this destruction that we remember, resist, and refuse. The manifestation of our futures is thus a refusal to adhere to the colonial death drive, the settler impulse to spiritual and cultural annihilation. We resist our destruction by demonstrating how we live.

10. If we are alive, if we are to live, and if this living will be beautiful, then it is because our relationships have charted paths across time, becoming celestial in their electric parabolas, in the precession of a planet steadied though story, made kin through song, relationships coursing through barren gulches, atop cresting waves, captured in codices that hold these patterns as constellations, the story of a woman's tears, the warmth of an ember carried across generations that illuminates our hearts in relation. That vibration is what makes the living dance.

Remnants and Relations

I want to remember, but some parts of myself are but remnants. This is what it means to be an Indian sometimes. We live as an assemblage of fragments, those remnants and relations that remain, lingering on the edge of oblivion, because of colonialism, time, neglect, insecurity, fear. And yet . . .

I remember reading James Mooney's *Myths of the Cherokee*, a document produced for the Smithsonian's Bureau of American Ethnology in 1900. Reading these stories because I craved the knowledge that I had been denied because of the circumstances of my life—because of colonialism. I read and I did not understand. I read again and could not follow. I tried to pry open those stories and find a kernel of authenticity, a truth for myself that I seemingly could not access.

Because this manifesto is about of the endurance of Indigenous kinship systems, knowledge, and love, I want to conclude with a letter to that younger me. I have so much to tell him, so much relating to do:

You don't have to figure it all out. You don't have to know everything right now. The process will become part of you, is you. The process is you learning from others, listening and associating your story with stories you hear and read and discuss and dream. That will define you, your storying. Not knowing is where you are now. But that does not define the totality of you, at least not forever. You will come to know the story of creation and its variations; the story of fire; the story of the Pine Tree and the Pleiades. You will come to have a predilection for certain themes: the liminal beings like Dayunisi, Water Beetle, who dove to the bottom of the endless sea to bring back a piece of mud that would become Elohi, the Middle World. Dayunisi will call to you because they span multiple worlds, a connector of realms. You, in your in-betweenness, will identify with those liminal beings who hold a special place in the Cherokee cosmos: Water Beetle, Water Spider, Bat, Flying Squirrel. You will see that others have also felt this way. Daniel Heath Justice's article "Towards a Theory of Anomaly" will be transformational for you.[19] You will see how you are not alone—not alone, for there are others who are drawn to such magic, to the marvelous transgressors who keep sacred truths, to stories about what happens at the interstices between bodies, worlds, and beings. You will start to feel those stories, internalize them, and realize that the storying of you, your becoming Cherokee, is part of a lifelong process. In fact, you will only later comprehend that all Cherokees are engaged in that same process. Aren't we all engaged in this ongoing process of relating through story, which is ceremony, which is knowledge, which is culture, which is spirituality? There is no end result of this storying, only an emergent series of becomings, or perhaps an iterative set of enactments of reciprocity—you will come to call this "speculative relations" in a book you are called to write.

You don't know all this yet, but you will think that because you have read this story, rather than learned it as a child around a fire or from an elder, you are somehow inauthentic. How many Cherokees first learned one of their own stories from a book? This is not a rhetorical question. With the ongoing colonialism—boarding schools, adoption, relocation programs, etc.—many Cherokees have learned our stories from a book rather than from a person. You will not realize this until later, but it will come as a revelation to you. Not just that you were not alone—even though you were so alone—but that your image of yourself was itself a projection, a specter of the Indian you thought you should have been, and yet could never become.

You will try to imagine what it was like before. You will obsess over the details of the lives of ancestors you will never know. The hard part is not imagining what their lives would have been like—enough graves have been unearthed, ethnographies written, testimonies recorded. Enough lives have been reconstructed through the eyes of white men for you to have a sense of what it would have been like to live under the sign of imminent destruction. You will read the testimony of the Trail of Tears and you will learn the names of the children who died: "Corn Tassel's child," "Oolahneta's child," "Nancy Bigbears Grand child [sic]," Goddard's Grand child [sic]," "Rainfrogs, or Lucy Redsticks [sic] daughter," Alsey Timberlakes Daughter of Charles Timberlake [sic]."[20] Or rather, you will realize that these children's names were not recorded, but that they did have names. They were loved. They are buried along winding paths, under mulberry trees, or else near a frozen stream.

The hard part is not a lack of forensic evidence, but the imaginative capacity to see a smile on the face that belongs to a jawbone held in a museum, or a caress on the skin of a woman whose care you can only glean from gestures embodied by kin, who themselves only knew kindness in dreams, or in memory.

But this is what I want to say: You are enough. You are enough. You are enough. You have all the tools you need to thrive in this world. You will be haunted, yes, by the specters of prejudice and inauthenticity and the hollow projections of a world you thought true, but which, even if it were, you cannot return to. You will live with those hauntings, find yourself in the presence of your own ghosts, and relate.

You will come to believe that the speculative relations you must navigate are not just of the past, but also of the future, those remnants that embed themselves into you, thorns, splinters of a world that no longer exists, and yet that you still strive to honor, to humbly work for its return somehow. Not a return to the pre-colonial life that has by now become a caricature, but to the freedom and fullness of Indigenous life, in all its complications and multi-facetedness, in its complex alchemy.

Living the fullness of your life is a service to others—this is what is required of you, in fact, because you are required for the fullness of the world. This world is diminished without you. This world is not whole, not balanced, without the entirety of your being, your queerness, your desires, your flesh, your radiance. This world is incomplete without the relations that you make possible because of the gifts you give freely. Those gifts are the service you offer, the hope of endurance, the possibility made real of a world that desperately needs you, that aches for you to make it whole.

Let me say this again: this world is incomplete without you. Again, this does not mean that the world revolves around you, but that its revolution is calibrated to include you, and if you are not there, giving your gifts, bearing yourself into the future, then the world will tilt, out of balance, off kilter. The gifts you bring, what you humbly offer, are your fierce dedication to others, your perseverance, your skill, your light. You bring that light and you do not diminish it, for the world, the functioning of the relations that make this world possible, depends on it. Plenitude requires you.

Is it too much to ask that this be a speculative manifestation of the lives we were meant to lead? Is it too much to ask of them, to bear witness to the writing of this, even in its inevitable failure? Perhaps the point is not to ask what we have been, but what we could be, what lives we can share if only we relate. If only we reach out and touch, knowing that the land has always been our first and abiding sensation. The first and abiding love we share.

What I mean is, you are loved because the land loves you.

JOSEPH M. PIERCE

If we knew the word for *relative* in every Indigenous
language, then what futures would we hold dear?

The beautiful world dances the stumbles.
The beautiful world dances dancing.

JANAÍNA OLIVEIRA

A Manifesto for Curation

JANAÍNA OLIVEIRA

> ... you have to dance dancing.
>
> JORGE BEN (1974)

In 1974, Jorge Ben, now Ben Jor, released *A Tábua de Esmeralda*, a unique album dedicated to the principles of alchemy. A tribute to Hermes Trismegistus and those who, like him, wanted to fly among the stars and live on a "planet of impossible possibilities."

Ben brings to his work a combination that has made him one of the central figures in Brazilian music. An alchemist himself, he began mixing in the mid-sixties the bourgeois chords of bossa nova with the cadences of soul, opening new paths for Black presence in the country's musical scene. The first step was to pay homage to Thoth—the Egyptian god whom the Romans decoded as Hermes Trismegistus, inventor of writing and alchemy, author of a manifesto on the dynamics of the world's creation. In the album's first moments, we hear the informal sound of conversations and some instructions given by Ben, who, like a good herald of new times, warns: "You have to dance dancing."

The insistent tautology of the verb *dance* reverberates as an exaltation of one of the fundamental alchemical principles: that of adaptability expressed in the fluidity of the water element.

Dancing while dancing means putting yourself in motion, at your own rhythm, which flows with the music and even without it. Dancing while dancing is the beginning of Ben's album and also of this manifesto, as it was through "dancing dancing" that cinema curation came into my life. In my case, dancing while dancing speaks to the non-linear paths off the many crossroads that led me to curate cinema. It doesn't say so much about a dimension of improvisation but rather about the necessary fluidity required of a Black woman in the Global South, to move through these domains of cinema and curation and transform the markers relegated by the colonial world to the margins—woman/Black/Global South—into power.

Dancing while dancing embodies the "poetics of trembling" that Édouard Glissant talks about. It is not about fear or uncertainty, nor is it a form of paralysis. Trem*bling,* or *tremblement* as insists Glissant, is "the instinctual feeling that we must refuse all categories of fixed and imperial thought. *Tremblement* is thinking in which we can lose time, lose time searching, in which we can wander, and in which we can counter all the systems of terror, domination, and imperialism with the poetics of *trembling*—it allows us to be in real contact with the world and with the peoples of the world." Behold then Glissant's "thought of trembling": "An instinct, an intuition of the world that we can't achieve with imperial thoughts, with thoughts of domination, thoughts of a systematic path toward a truth that we've posited in advance. It's metaphorical, but it's also real, concrete."[1]

In the alchemical link that mixes Glissant with Ben Jor, part of the poetics of trembling and dancing are the encounters that happen in whirlwinds. These encounters have brought me here in the formulation of this manifesto, which, like all manifestos, aims for some degree of guidance, but in this case, is anything but a formula. Dancing while dancing means being permanently open to the stability of the unstable, embracing constant risks, and understanding that the successes are in the process, not the results. Repeating Glissant: it is "metaphorical, but it is also concrete." The concreteness lies in the urgent epistemological shifts (epistemology understood in a broader sense, including other possibilities of knowledge beyond just the rational) in the ways of thinking about cinema and the world.

In 2023, Martinique filmmaker Wally Fall released his second feature film, a film-experiment that reflects intimately on mental health issues in conjunction with Bèlè music and dance, the country's leading cultural form of expression. I could bring in Fall's film as another component to the alchemy of this manifesto, but for now I want only its title to reverberate: *Mantjé Tonbé Sé Viv*. The literal translation from Creole is "almost stumbling is life," but the poetic title used for the film's international circulation is "Dancing the Stumble."

With this image, I invite you to dance in this manifesto, making the necessary shifts to think about cinema curation for the beautiful world. The beautiful world dances the stumbles. The beautiful world dances dancing.

I

Care, cultivation, healing. These are the meanings to which the etymological origins of the word *curatorship* point, coming from the Latin term *curare*.[2] The etymology of the word *curation* as care was often evoked primarily in the context of reflections on the visual arts. These are formulations that have emerged in the world of exhibitions in museums, galleries, and biennials, especially in the second half of the twentieth century, due to the increasingly constant use of the term.[3] Harald Szeemann, Swiss curator responsible for *documenta 5* in 1972, was known for expanding the notion of curator from a mere manager of objects to a creator of ideas, and was one of the first to point out the connection between curation and the notion of care.[4] But, as fellow curator Kate Fowle reminds us, the possible meanings contained in the Latin word include one notion of curation that unfolds in the English as a gesture of keeping, taking care of something or someone, or even as the act of supervising.[5] Thus, by extension, curators are guardians, protectors, and conservators (in every sense of the word) of artistic expressions and values.

Be that as it may, present in all paths of meaning is a hierarchy, a dimension of power implied at the root of the word and the activity of curation. The power resides in these caretaker-guardians' intermediation of the relationship and contact between artists, works, and the public. Curators are, therefore, mediators in their multiple variations—translators, conductors, connectors—acting as the contact between works and the public. In the hierarchical exercise of their functions, curators are responsible for choices that often influence the direction of works and artists, which impact the regimes of visibility and erasure that the art world perpetuates. Still, in this sense, curators can also be "the figure who stands in the middle of the way—an obstacle," as the Nigerian artist and curator Olu Oguibe said in the early 2000s.[6] It is noteworthy that in many cases, the constitutive instance of power present in curatorial practices shares its responsibilities with the institutions that house the curators, especially when it comes to the institutional limits and guidelines that are imposed. Although relevant, bringing institutionality into the equation contextualizes but does not reduce the role of *gatekeeper* that can be played.

It is not within the scope of this manifesto to retrace the entire genealogy of transformations and crises that curatorial activity has gone through and is going through in the world of arts—from the specialist dilettante or erudite art historian dedicated to a particular era or style, to the curator affiliated with institutions and the emergence of the independent curator. However, for the purposes of this manifesto, it is crucial to understand how curating in cinema develops not only in contact with but in dynamics very close to those of the visual arts. The tension (not to say rivalry) between the fields of cinema and museum is historic, as are the confluences between them. These are crossed paths, especially from the moment that cinema begins to enter the museum space (in the same way that works previously restricted to museums start to enter the cinema space). The year of Szeemann's *documenta 5* was also the year that the Cannes Film Festival abandoned selection based on representation by country and instead delegated artistic direction and film selection to a programming committee. This model has been adopted for the majority of international festivals, "inaugurating a growing accumulation of curatorial power in the hands of the director and programmers."[7]

The trajectory of cinema curating thus follows that of art curating. Akin to the field of visual arts, wherein art historians and scholars became curators, in hegemonic cinema circuits, critics and cinephiles became curators. In a similar way, the growing and inevitable digitalization of life, which restructured borders and shortened temporalities, also impacted perceptions and curatorial activities both in the world of arts, which began to feel these transformations at the beginning of the 2000s, and in the context of cinema, which in turn echoed these changes around a decade later. One of the pragmatic effects of these changes was the increase in the number of people carrying out curatorial activities, causing what Kate Fowle called "an identity crisis. Curating is now an industry, constructing its own history as it evolves. At the same time, it is an increasingly multifaceted practice that gives rise to much speculation as to how it functions and what it entails." Along with this crisis, a statement has become common in the worlds of both the visual arts and cinema: "now everyone is a curator."

It is impossible to ignore the tone of discontent implicit in this statement. A tone that makes one feel that the notion of curation as care is no stronger than the pacts that this task has with the notion of power and, mainly, with the place of privilege from which this practice is usually exercised. "The job of a curator is loaded with assumptions of class privilege and cultural capital," says Kemi Adeyemi in her "Brief Oral History of the Recent Past" on Black women curators.[8] Therefore, to join this select group, you need, at least, some degree of financial autonomy to be able to afford (or survive) the reality of poorly paid internships and early career salaries or the opportunities that arise in volunteer activities.

Here, perhaps, there is a slight difference between the world of curating in visual arts and the world of curating in cinema: with the proliferation of digital media and, more recently, online film exhibitions, independent curatorial initiatives with less elitist origins emerge. It's urgent to explore and consider these new presences in the field and their contributions. For now, let us keep in mind that the curatorial activity bears as its mark a classist history, and by extension, one that is sexist and racist—as we have already learned from Black feminist thinkers, we cannot deal with the developments of capitalism without intersecting them with race and gender.

In this manifesto, as part of the strategies for a beautiful world, it is essential not to overly detail the dimensions of power involved in the curatorial processes. This perspective must always be kept on the horizon, as for a large number of populations from non-hegemonic territories around the world, cinema curation, instead of meaning care, creates and perpetuates trauma. These are traumas resulting from the epistemic violence that essayist Gayatri Spivak writes of when discussing the damage caused to subalternate subjectivities by the colonial imposition of identities.[9] These are traumas that extend from the repeated objectification and *tokenization* present in images, whether in negative or positive stereotypes, as even the affirmative character of a positive image is a form of generalization that encapsulates what is singular in everything that exists.[10]

Such traumas developed from multiple absences and erasures. I remember bell hooks in "The Oppositional Gaze" and the process she described: how Black women, to exist *with* cinema—that is, in a world of which films are a part—needed to create spaces of agency, since historically no place was intended for them, either on the screen or in the audience. "Conventional representations of Black women have done violence to the image," says hooks; "to this assault, many Black women spectators shut out the image, looked the other way, accorded cinema no importance in their lives." According to hooks, all the women she spoke to who, out of love for cinema, insisted on continuing to watch films "had to close their own critique, analysis; they had to forget racism. And mostly, they did not think about sexism."[11] Watching movies shouldn't be such a painful thing.

Moreover, traumas have been updated by the exponential commoditization of Black presence in the arts and cinema. "All my ancestors have been sold / That's probably why my music sells," sings Baco Exu do Blues, a Brazilian musician quoted by artist and thinker Jota Mombaça in her text "The Cognitive Plantation." And she adds: "Since the commodification of this perspective—our perspectives—depend[s] directly on a certain continuity between our artistic production and our social-historical place, maybe it makes sense to state that the selling of our music, texts, ideas and images reenacts, as a historical tendency, the regimes of acquisition of Black bodies that established the predicament of Blackness at the core of the world as we know it."[12]

The traumas reiterated and updated by moving images undermine the confidence of those who watch them in such a way that work is needed to reconstruct these imaginaries, so that death, violence, and oblivion are not automatically identified as places of belonging. It is no coincidence that in many of the so-called peripheries of the world, populations have long recognized cinema as a space they could not frequent. In a recent speech given in the city of Rio de Janeiro, Françoise Vergès posed the question: "How does the spirit of resistance survive despite erasure?"[13]

A brief pause in the dance steps. Let's let this question reverberate a little.

It is urgent that, in cinema, curation as care abandons the historically constituted rhetorical and elitist plane and transforms itself into something else. It is critical that curation as care becomes epistemology, as a problem for thinking along the lines of what Christina Sharpe posits.[14] Now that the minimum reconnaissance of the room has been done, let's take the first steps. Our dance begins here.

II

But what does it mean to make care a problem for curation? The first thing to say is that cinema curation based on an epistemology of care follows paths other than the "old cinephilia," that is to say the traditional canon of cinema in the Global North as stated by Girish Shambu in his manifesto "For a New Cinephilia." Having care as an epistemic key to curatorial practices requires a shift in the way of thinking about films, screenings, exhibitions, and festivals. It is to consider them not autonomously, as phenomena in themselves, isolated from the world and shielded by the category of universality of art that Western thought values so much. Films, sessions, exhibitions, and festivals are in the world, just like we are. As says Shambu, "no matter how ardent and passionate our love for this medium, the world is bigger and vastly more important than cinema."[15]

The old cinephilia, which primarily supports the hegemonic thinking about curating, still resonates today, in the twenty-first century, as a defense of the autonomy of art. The old cinephiles resent the mass production that dominates modernity, and they desperately want to have back the world where it was possible to say solely and exclusively that films mattered. They are orphans of the auratic era of exclusivism, both for those who produce and those who speak about these images. They use this aura as a shield for choices. They claim themselves impartial, but they are in fact manipulators who pretend to be invisible in power dynamics. They re-enact the debates on the polarizations that separate form and content, aesthetics from politics, instead of questioning the meaning of operating in conceptual pairs and dualisms. Again and again, they repeat: "Now anyone does curation." They demonstrate the imposition of rhythm instead of letting themselves be carried away by the sound. The problem is that when (and if) they like to dance, they only know how to do it to the music they compose.

The invitation to dance that this manifesto constitutes is a way of breaking out of this rigidity and moving toward a thought of cinema or cinephilia in terms of po/ethics (poethics) that Denise Ferreira da Silva and Rizvana Bradley talk about:

> In contradistinction to understandings of the artwork as an autonomous totality, or those that would consign the artwork to some iteration of Kant's *forma finalis*—that is, the reductive ascription of a formal purposiveness to the object—a poetic reading stresses the provisional ground where questions of form, formlessness, and abstraction collide.[16]

An unstable terrain that shakes, where you need to know how to stumble. A terrain in which curating is unhesitatingly assumed as an extended experience that expands the curator's activity beyond research, selection, and programming of films. The notion of care-as-epistemology requires this proud extension of understanding of the curatorial activity. And I say *proud* because those old cinephiles will contend in a very derogatory way that this amplification beyond the films is close to what the contemporary post-production process of a film is: a kind of cheat, a falsification of the fundamental artistic gesture of the author. According to German film historian Thomas Elsaesser, curation as post-production is comparable to the extraction of natural resources: what it harvests is the exhibition value, and what it extracts is a celebrity.[17] From this perspective, in addition to a change in power relations, there would also be a transformation in the way the film is shown in which the dimension of care would be exchanged for that of "appropriation."

Here, prioritizing the centrality of the film to the detriment of everything else—but above all, the public—appears once again. It's as if films weren't meant to be seen, or at least not by everyone. In a slip of the spirals of time, we almost have the sensation of returning to the beginning of the Industrial Revolution in Europe and the heated disputes between popular culture and erudition, or how to cultivate (another possible meaning for *curare*) the modern subject amidst the world of the masses. The defense of curation as care is about caring for films, artists, and the auteur cinema circuit, not just the public.

This manifesto's proposal recovers and reaffirms this curatorial perspective, which is not restricted to reflecting on the films themselves. Here, care is not a defense of the exceptional but of the *singularity* of the works. The challenging question is how to take care of the uniqueness of the films and how to display them in contexts that enhance their relationships and contacts without falling into the traps of transparency in Western thought, which either exoticizes or generalizes human experiences due to the need for understanding. The task of the curator who considers care-as-epistemology when dealing with films focuses largely on defending the right to opacity, as claimed by Édouard Glissant—the right to forms of existence and film cultures other than that of the old cinephilia. Traditional and canonical ways of seeing, thinking about, and curating films will continue to thrive, but, henceforth, at least in non-hierarchical coexistence with other possibilities of understanding cinema and the world.

III

For whom are films curated and programmed? This seemingly basic question is fundamental to this manifesto. When analyzing the bibliographies produced on curating, whether in the visual arts or cinema, it becomes clear that this "whom" is sidelined or simply absent from the debate. In addition to the films, there needs to be a fundamental care for audiences. We need to think about the public. So I come back to the question: What does it mean to make care a problem for curators in the beautiful world? The answer is neither unique nor certain. *Mantjé tonbé sé viv*—it's almost by falling that you live. It's about taking risks, betting on what the multiple dimensions of care-as-thought bring to curatorial practices. At this point, one must take the risk of pointing out possible definitions of care. At this point, the seemingly solitary dance becomes collective, creating crossroads between thoughts and curatorial practices.

In a profound way, Tina Campt's reflections in the second edition of *Loophole of Retreat: Venice* resonate with the foundational notion of care-as-thought:

> Care is comfort, compassion, and sustainability delivered even in the face of inevitable failure. Care is a demonstration and instantiation of attachment and relationship. Care is also a refusal. It is a refusal to be insensitive to the pain or suffering of others. It is a refusal to look away or look past the precarity of those in need.[18]

Care is presented here as an epistemology that refuses to be indifferent to the multiple traumas of coloniality. Care that will permeate both the viewing of films and the understanding of the historical-social structures and dynamics when programming them in the extended experience of a curatorial proposal. None of what is being said here is new. Anyone who works as a film curator is aware of these issues concerning audience profiles and the characteristics of venues with their demographic and regional markers. Curating for the beautiful world implies equating unapologetically the status between the aesthetics and formal aspects of the works with the dimensions of everyday life.

Instantiating links and relationships. Again: it's metaphorical, but it's also real, concrete. In the same way that practices that reiterate traumas continue to exist, there are more and more examples of exhibitions, festivals, collectives of programmers, and publications that are guided by what I call curatorial care-as-thought. It is no coincidence that most of these initiatives originate in territories and/or cultures historically crossed by the aforementioned erasures, invisibilizations, and stereotyping: the South and the Global East; people who identify as Black, brown, Indigenous, Latino, or Asian; the LGBTQIA+ community. Groups that refuse to watch passively as the grammar of violence, to use Saidiya Hartman's expression,[19] is reiterated in moving images and their circuits. To dance dancing, a concrete metaphor for the poetics of trembling, permeates the thoughts of those who live on the margins.

I could mention here the creation of POC2 (Programmers of Colour Collective), announced at the 2019 Sundance Festival, which "advocate[s] for a more inclusive programming pool worldwide" and currently has almost 370 members. Or the emergence of the Cousin Collective, an initiative that brings together North American Indigenous directors and curators. Originated in the aftermaths of the 2018 edition of the Flaherty Film Seminar, the future members of the Collective first gathered to protest against the Seminar's logo, which featured the silhouette of the protagonist of *Nanook of the North*, a 1922 film by Robert Flaherty, considered to be a pioneer in film history but also a champion of the adverse treatment of Indigenous Peoples in cinema.

Or, going east, the creation of the digital journal *Curatography—The Study of Curatorial Culture*, produced by Curating Asia International (CAI). This Taipei-based network brings together curators, artists, art educators, and cultural workers from and for Asia. "Curation in the twenty-first century is marked not only by its expanding role in society but also by its changing functions and responsibilities.

The neologism 'curatography' is thus born out of the necessity to retroactively define shifting meanings of 'curator' and 'curation.'[20]

Speaking from a Brazilian experience, I could point out, for example, the CachoeiraDoc Documentary Film Festival. Created during the expansion of public universities outside the country's metropolis by President Lula in his first mandate, the University of the Recôncavo Bahia (UFRB) is now considered one of the advanced centers of cinema in the country. During its eight years of existence, the festival represented a critical and crucial approach to the national film context—a kind of "healing by the margins," as stated by curator, UFRB professor, and festival founder Amaranta César. For her, CachoeiraDoc adopted:

> the idea of recognition, rather than judgment, as a guiding principle for the research and selection of films in our curatorial exercise. This conceptual movement sought to give theoretical substance to the need to embrace the desire for visibility and listening of the multiple new film subjects that have emerged in Brazil in recent years and their effects on our critical practice.[21]

The festival was a breeding ground for reflections that served as inspiration to this manifesto's claims. It was at the 2016 Festival that the first systematically organized discussion about film curation in Brazil took place. The event, "Curatorship from the Woman's Perspective," was a two-day immersion that paved the way for these formulations of care as an epistemology, as a question for curatorial thinking in cinema.

Bringing my curatorial practice into this reflection-manifesto, another example of what I call here the curation of care would be Opacity, a program I put together for the sixty-sixth edition of the Flaherty Film Seminar in 2021.[22] Due to the global COVID-19 pandemic, the Seminar was held remotely for the first time in its history, which added even more layers to the thought of care. In addition to the challenge of programming an event for an online audience, we were already in the second year of the pandemic and exhausted from looking at our computer screens. From the beginning, I was interested in proposing a program that would work as a kind of displacement of the dominant notions of cinephilia. There were many paths that helped me reach the Seminar's final form. Isaac Julien's work had been on the horizon from the moment I began working on this project; Julien is part of a generation of filmmakers who have influenced me in so many ways. He also came to mind because of his relationship with Okwui Enwezor, an essential point of reference for me as a curator. I was particularly inspired by his curation of the *documenta 11* art exhibition in 2002, which reflected on *créolité*, Caribbean culture, and changing canons. Enwezor's propositions for that exhibition deeply impacted how I think about cinema and curation.

The desire to work with artists from cinematic experiences and landscapes that are frequently unrepresented was a determining factor; my intention was always to work with non-white artists. The challenge was bringing these works and reflections together without falling into frameworks of exoticizing or showing them as only "other" to the white, Western norm. I wanted to put together a curatorial proposal that echoed a move toward liberation.

Glissant thought of opacity as a radical defense of the singularity of all things, as well as a refusal of the Western logic of total transparency that reduces everything to only what can be understood or known. The curatorial proposal for Opacity was an invitation into a sort of displacement, a discomfort from leaving behind the expectations of the dominant world of cinema—of explaining and knowing everything. The Flaherty Seminar was, in some ways, an ideal place for this. Opacity suggested a way to leave behind the rigid, Western ways of experiencing cinema and the traditional canon, of traveling unexpected paths and exploring other possibilities and modes of perception of the cinematic experience.

The entire program consisted of nineteen distinct sessions that spanned ten days. While the seminar is usually only one week long, we extended it to accommodate different time zones. We had four hundred people attending from forty-two countries. It's important to note that I was not developing a linear argument with the objective of "understanding" what opacity is. On the contrary, every session spiraled back to the same statement about opacity from a different perspective. Always the same, but different. This was one of the primary keys to how the program was shaped.

In keeping with this expanded way of thinking about curatorship, I took into consideration translation dynamics and how best to accommodate the many artists who didn't speak English as their original language. From the development of the online platform to the curating of the moderators, together with Samara Chadwick, the Seminar's executive director, I ensured that multiple layers of care would echo. In their entire careers, Opacity was the first time that Brazilian Indigenous filmmakers Sueli Maxacali and Isael Maxacali had taken part in an event speaking their original language, as it was of the utmost importance to all that their speeches be given in a language of thought inherent to their creative practice, which often happened in the form of songs. In one of the last debates of the Seminar, a film by the Maxacalis, *Yãmĩyhex, the Women-Spirit*, was shown together with *Insan (Human Being)*, a 1994 film by Sudanese filmmaker and member of the Sudanese Film Group Ibrahim Shaddad. Between the cities of Teófilo Otoni, in the hinterland of Minas Gerais, from which Sueli and Isael spoke, and Khartoum, where the members of the Sudanese Film Group and their Arabic translator were, an incredible debate took place, moderated by Almudena Escobar López, a Spanish curator who was in New York at the time. The barriers of language, a primordial dimension of colonial domination, were overcome, further enhancing reflection on the films and moving the audiences from different parts of the world.

There are many ways of assuming that curating is a "radical act of care," to quote the title of a beautiful program organized by Greg de Cuir Jr. for the Media City Film Festival in 2020. Addressing the issue of translation in the conversations that accompany the films is one such act. Still, there are curators and programmers who believe that this concern is not part of their duties, relegating it to the institutions. To give true attention to language and translation issues is just one of the many layers of curation as care. Not delegating or assuming the possibilities of the actual scope of action allows other epistemologies and ways of knowledge to flourish in different film cultures and have space in the cinema world.

IV

Finally, it could be argued that the clamor of this manifesto revolves solely and exclusively around demands for representation and representativeness, encompassing issues such as ethics in the production and circulation of films and the presence of diverse people on programming and curatorial committees, as has been largely translated in recent debates on "curatorial justice" held at major festivals in recent years. Yet I don't think the pairing of these terms *curatorship* and *justice* is ideal, not only because it detaches our understanding of curatorship; we would also need to rethink what we mean by justice, as there is no doubt that representation and representativeness are central issues in any contemporary cinema debate. But we also need to recognize that the fight for representation doesn't necessarily mean an end to erasure or some form of equity.

It is, therefore, a question of not underestimating the clamor for representation and representativeness while at the same time valuing the demand for maintaining the singularities of experiences. Part of the challenge of care-as-thought for curation is creating possibilities for coexistence. It is necessary to consider that a direct leap beyond representation and representativeness can only be made by those who have somehow "overcome" trauma, who recognize it as a constitutive dimension but don't want to be limited to it, those who "articulate a method of encountering a past that is not past," to use Christina Sharpe's words.[23] For some audiences, filmmakers, and curators, dealing with representation is what matters, and that's fine. But let's not forget, as Glissant tells us in the manifesto he wrote with Patrick Chamoiseau, "all regeneration emerges from disruption."[24] So this manifesto urges us to keep dancing dancing, to navigate unapologetically and fearlessly the trembling and its abyss.

V

In the middle of the tribute tracks to Hermes Trismegistus, on side B of *A Tábua de Esmeralda*, we listen to Jorge Ben sing "Zumbi," an ode to the revolutionary leader of the Quilombo dos Palmares—a maroon community that resisted the forces of the Portuguese empire in the northeast of Brazil for almost a century. After telling us about the history of slavery in Brazil, Ben sings: "I want to see what happens when Zumbi gets here. What is going to happen."

I'll finish here with Zumbi's song because curation in the beautiful world implies practices of resistance and fugitivity. It's about escaping through the gaps, dribbling, and making things work despite institutional limitations, budgets, and film politics: that is, to dance dancing. That's what care-as-thought requires us to do.

I'm not thinking or practicing this manifesto alone. It's a collective enterprise; it's about togetherness.

So yes, now everyone is a curator. It's like that in the beautiful world.

JANAÍNA OLIVEIRA

The beautiful world dances the stumbles.
The beautiful world dances dancing.

How can we move beyond this horizon
to a place we've never been?

PHOEBE BOSWELL

Manifesto of the As Yet Unlived Thing

PHOEBE BOSWELL

Allow me to take us back.
It is 2020, and the world has just broke broke.
(We all remember.)
It is 2020 and the news is never good.

It is 2020 and I have not seen anyone for eight weeks. I am delirious, bewildered, and aimless, unless the sole aim is simply not going entirely mad. It is 2020 and the government has decided that people like me, those with the most unruly bodies, those deemed most at risk of dying from Covid must "shield," must remove ourselves entirely from society—no food shops, no daily walks—until it is deemed safe enough to once again breathe communal air. They have done the deathly mathematics and decided, in a rush, to sequester the weak and keep capitalism strong. They deliver this message via a text so dystopian it knocks the air flat out of my chest. They promise weekly care packages, which begin to show up on my doorstep, and I take what I need and leave the rest outside for my neighbors to help themselves to. My neighbors in turn set up a mutual aid system to run outside errands for people like me, and I realize that, bar sideways hellos in the elevator after long days or brief notes on the weather as we fumble for our keys, this is the most interaction we've had in my eight years of living in this tower block.

I make a vow to save this in future times because interdependence is liberating and this London living can make you cold. Alone, I dedicate my days to Korean skincare and chapati-making, which I'd promised myself prior to the pandemic to make my love language. If I love you, I will make you chapatis and we will eat them hot, straight from the pan. I imagine myself as some sort of Adrian Piper, sequestering in *Food for the Spirit*, and it is somewhat romantic and somewhat artistic and I imagine that this could be something of a transformative moment towards reaching some sort of miraculous new understanding of myself, how I relate to my body and to the world outside. My body *becomes* world. I nourish it. I lather it in creams and potions and massage it. I stroke my own skin. I feed it porridge in the morning and drink enough water. I walk up the five steps to my front door and down again countless times a day and my sister Freddie and I commit to doing YouTube Pilates via FaceTime, and dance sessions, and long, bewildered conversations that turn to pixels through our mobile phones. I consider reaching out to long lost lovers, or attempting to find new ones, to risk it all via video chat. Separate and together, we all have to seek out new ways to engage. Skype has fumbled its bag and Zoom becomes household. The sky outside my window becomes companion. On foggy days I suffer most. I swear the postman starts to wear more aftershave than usual because the days he comes I relish smelling him through the slit in the door, perfume drifting in reminding me that other humans exist, and are heroic, and smell really, *really* nice.

———

I receive an invitation from the outside world.

It is early in the pandemic still, and like most things, art operations have ceased and our studios are off-limits. In Nottingham, a show I was due to open is abandoned two days into install, right after the technicians unload: *Transit Terminal*, a sculptural drawing consisting of twelve charcoal figures, each occupying a totemic purpose-built box 7 ft x 2 ft x 1 ft, the standard dimensions of an average adult coffin turned upright. The figures, drawn onto the backs of the boxes with their backs to us, stand seemingly in limbo between here and somewhere else, some unknown place. Their stillness is juxtaposed by a flock of chalky migratory birds in flight, drawn onto the black interior of each box. I made the installation in 2014, to address global migration and notions of (un)freedom, uprootedness, and refusal, in response to an avoidable tragedy in which five hundred people drowned off the coast of Lampedusa. And now here they stand in the gallery, mid-pandemic, waiting for the world to re-announce itself. Silent ghosts, waiting. I begin to wonder what the unknown place is, in this context, and if we'll ever find it, and how long before we get there.

And then this invitation.

Some art people are coming together to build a virtual art museum, a place to exist online which we can all visit in this moment of limbo and ennui, where we can satisfy our cravings to be with art, to stand surrounded by it, within it, a possibility that has been taken from us by way of global crisis. They sell this to me as a state-of-the-art innovation project in which they will collaborate with top architects, technologists, gamers, and coders to create a fully interactive space of imagination and wonder. The reason they are getting in touch with me, they say, is to see if I want to be the museum's inaugural "artist-in-residence." Sitting at home, face mask on, chapati on stove, I start to imagine what might be possible within such a premise. Imagine! A space that is virtual, but situated within this time when so much of our lives have necessarily moved online, as to render the separation between the online and irl somewhat blurred. This space, virtual so all the logistical implications of creating an immersive installation could be bypassed. No need for economy of thought based on cost, on scale, on the limitations of physical technologies like light beams from projectors that blind one's eyes or TV screens that add this jarring reminder of plastic to what could otherwise be this illusionary, beautiful fever dream. Even gravity wouldn't matter in this place. We could fly. We could soar. In this virtual space, in the midst of this global pandemic where everything is skewed and up for reimagining, we could dream.

Right before the pandemic, I had gone to Zanzibar to our family home, to rest and gain energy from the swell of the Indian Ocean in preparation for a 2020 which was set to be super busy with travel, install, and exhibition commitments. I knew that once I got back to London post-holiday in mid-January, things would be non-stop workwise till November. I was excited, motivated, buzzing... A little nervous, honestly. Little did I know that we knew so little.

Anyway, I'm on the beach and I see in the distance this group of fishermen on the horizon, slowly, deftly coming up to shore. I recognize Cheupe and wave hello. The group comes up, exhausted after a long, difficult fishing expedition. I learn that the effects of global capitalism, overtourism, overfishing, and the climate crisis have affected their fishing practices; they now need to go further out and can no longer use the local dugout boats, the ngalawas, carved by generations of skilled hands out of wise wood from the island's tall palms, mango and cashew trees; they now have to use fiberglass ones and their journeys are becoming more treacherous.

Seeing them laden with their weapons, their catch, and makeshift protection from the elements, I begin to imagine this narrative that perhaps they'd been on some epic journey across the horizon line, in search of the unknown place, The New Place.

I start to think what this place might be, and how difficult it actually is to imagine a *new* place because our imaginations are so limited to what we already know—to the binds and rationale of our lived experience, right?

How can we know what is beyond the horizon? How can we move beyond this horizon to a place we've never been? To the as yet unlived, unexperienced thing?

In *Experiments in Imagining Otherwise*, Lola Olufemi asserts that "the way we talk about this life and living, the language we use, builds a kind of structure that turns the horizon (that point where potentiality meets the substance of our reality) into a mirage." As an example, Lola describes how

> when we say "housing for all" and the government responds with "the homeless are being temporarily housed in hotels to avoid the spread of the virus," they are building a linguistic structure that defines the realm of the possible, that simplistically tells us to want less, to expect that total reconfiguration is out of the question. Like a poorly designed building, linguistic structures affect how we

think, breathe, move, and act. The mould sticks to our skin. We are familiar with a particular kind of linguistic structure: the preservation of a system of organisation that places capital before all else. This system ties our hands and feet together.[1]

This system is what we can see when we gaze out to the edge of the horizon. Zoé Samudzi asserts that "decolonisation is a horizon, decolonisation has no end."[2] These fishermen in Zanzibar, I'm proposing in speculation, have sailed out beyond it. They are our Future Ancestors, in search of the something new.

I had already begun to draw from this encounter in the days just prior to the pandemic, building up the narrative through drawing semi-imagined portrait drawings based on that East African beach. I was thinking of the glisten of sweat/ of salt/of memory, the way each kiss and sting the skin. I was thinking how to get pastel to do that. How to do it with pencil on a page. I was thinking of Glissant, of errantry, of exile; of snorkels and goggles and seeing and breathing underwater; of the way the eye involuntarily creases to avoid the glare from the sun. I was thinking about the sun. The velvet caress of the breeze off the reef and the ancestral power of that equatorial sun. I was thinking about freedom, what it is and what it isn't, and what it looks like to gaze back. I was reintroducing color into my work after many years of being resolutely monochromatic. I was thinking of color as a portal. I was thinking of the unrepentant insistence of tides and the buoyancy of water and the remedial nature of floating. I was thinking of new worlds, of beyond worlds, of organizing, and community, and unfettered curiosity.

Back to the invitation: imagining a new place seemed more imperative than ever now. Perhaps this virtual space could become an exploration ground, imagining where those fishermen might have gone beyond the horizon and the limits of our known reality.

Perhaps this project could conjure something that pushed at the oblique limits of my own imagination, my own horizon, into the spirit world of something new, somewhere otherwise. As prison abolitionist Mariame Kaba writes, we are going to need "a million experiments."

I say a resounding yes.

Time passes.

I'm sent another text message from the government, this time saying their computer was actually wrong, that I am not actually on the list, I was never actually meant to shield, and that they will therefore no longer be sending me care packages. Again, they have done some maths. I'm overwhelmed, disoriented, let down, confused, and honestly frightened to leave the house. It is too much, it has been too much, it was all too much, wasn't it? The witnessing, the grief, the rage, the impossible loss, the chaotic temporality.

Those first images of Italian medics donning protective clothing to enter the homes of the sick, and the dead being buried hastily in mass graves with no family to guide their journeys / Death showing up relentless and obstinate on the news / Those daily updates from deathly figures of deathly figures of those dead and those dying but not quite dead and on respirators of which hospitals simply did not have enough / Chinese cities being built in days to house their sick / The racism against East Asians that ensued from the onslaught of massive and state-driven conspiracy / How we were being told at first that the virus was not affecting Black communities to the same extent as white ones, and then being told that of course it is, and more so, because suffering is structural, and why would this be any different / Those French scientists arrogantly announcing that they were going to test out their cures on African populations first / Those perplexed think pieces from Western journalists who simply could not understand why African populations on the continent were not dying to the same extent as Western ones / The messaging around mask-wearing being so erratic and nonsensical, relating more to the ill-planning of governments than to the care and the science of the matter, that if I cough and there's a molecule-resistant piece of cloth between me and you, it will transfer fewer particles to you, who has to breathe near me, your neighbor / The trickling down of ableist capitalist ideology that asserted that if you were old or had preconditions, it was somehow okay and understandable to see you die, when the truth was that Covid could disable and dispose of anyone / The images that circulated on social media of doctors and nurses with creased, haunted faces, working impossible shifts in tightly fitted masks worn too long / Stories of how so many of them moved out of their homes and into hotels so they wouldn't need to bring their contaminated bodies home to their loved ones / I remember phone calls with my Kenyan aunties who work in American care homes and were not being given appropriate PPE so instead were having to rely on potent ginger tea that they drank at quantity while wiping the asses of elderly Americans who refused to say thank you, not even in a pandemic / Remember being told in Britain to clap for our healthcare workers, outside our windows, banging pots and pans, and seeing politicians join in for the photo op while voting not to give them fair pay / Remember when gaunt politicians who never intended to follow their own rules told us that if we were in love or lust or not quite sure yet but not quite cohabiting yet we'd have to make quick decisions to be together or be apart, and we all had to determine who our most loved ones are, who we wished to have in our bubbles / Remember when they recommended doggystyle as the least threatening form of sex / Kissing should be limited, for obvious reasons. No one saw their grandparents, grandparents died in care homes at a criminal and devastating rate / We watched politicians lie point-blank, staring straight at us through our TV screens / We ordered more than we needed on Amazon just to feel something and we watched as billionaires got richer while small businesses and livelihoods collapsed / That mashup of anarchy, rage, and shame that churned in our bellies, knowing that *this* was the moment, that if shop stockers and food producers and rubbish collectors and healthcare workers *refused* to go to work that systems would very quickly collapse, but knowing too how much we were dependent on them for keeping us alive in that moment / We were told to wash our groceries / Wash our hands / We were taught how to wash our hands by singing Happy Birthday while lathering with warm water and soap, and we wondered how many people didn't wash their hands properly prior to a global pandemic / And then—we watched a white American police officer place his knee on the neck of a man named George Floyd in broad daylight. We counted how many times he said he could not breathe, and we saw him call for his mother. And we witnessed the world break, break anew. It was all too much and it has been too much and we've slowly been sinking still in this grief and this rage and the sinking is structural, and it is somatic, and it is related to systemic failings but it is deep, deep in the cracks and the fissures and the connective tissues of our bodies, and the cracks of the earth, its atmosphere, its emissions, and my stomach flips, flips for no reason now.

How much closer does the call have to get? How much collateral damage has to happen for the lessons we are going to need for the future? asks Stephen Jenkinson.[3]

Let me get back to the story. I receive the call that the museum has been built and it's time for my first "site visit." I'm given the link and I type it into my browser, it loads up and I find myself in this huge, cavernous space. It has walls. They are cold concrete. The ceilings are high. Slits in the walls cast dainty light beams onto polished concrete floors which I know I could slip on if I wasn't paying attention and that it would hurt. It is sleek. Industrial. Chic. I learn quickly how to navigate the controls and I turn to see what looks like a massive window, floor to ceiling, possibly sliding doors, outside of which is this idyllic patio of plants and flowers. In the distance I see what looks like a forest, and in front of it, a vast and glistening lake, so emerald-blue and fantastic I immediately want to move to it, to dive into it and float there. I move closer to the window, and as I do, the controls stop working, and the picturesque outside becomes merely pixels. I have gone too close, and they haven't worked that part out yet, you cannot *go* outside. You can't break the glass or gracefully glide through it and across the grass to reach the water. Fine. I turn and see a huge iron door that reaches the ceiling. It is grand and beautiful and sculpted and foreboding. I move towards it. As I do, the meticulously textured iron too begins to corrode into just another configuration of pixels. It is a door but you cannot open it, another edge of this virtual experience, and I am reminded of my own door, the one through which I smelled that postman's cologne all those days I was not allowed out either. Cool. It is still a work in progress. Excellent. I circle back to my initial position and start to move forward, almost immediately finding myself in "Gallery 1," the main gallery, a sprawling white cube in the center of the museum. Because coders are not curators, they have adorned the white walls with what I presume they downloaded when they googled "art," needing jpegs to demonstrate what the gallery would look like when hung with pictures. All around me: Picasso, Degas, Monet, Manet, dead white men taking up space in the central gallery, number one.

We move.

I hit another wall. The other edge of this world we are now in. Instinctively I turn left—have I been to this place before?—and find myself at the foot of a large marble staircase. How do you go up? I wonder. I'm told to just keep going straight with the controls. However, the movement is glitchy and it sticks on every step. I think about accessibility. My sister, who sometimes uses a wheelchair, rates a museum based on whether she can move around with ease. Large, bombastic spaces are tiring, and hard, so I'm always super conscious whenever I show anywhere that there's ease of movement and a place to sit. And here we are, in the full freedom of virtuality, and this place *fails* at access. It is *hard* to mount the stairs.

I trip. I stumble. I glitch. Eventually I get up to the top and immediately—another wall. Another preventative edge. *How is it that we're in a virtual space, and we keep bumping into actual non-actual actual walls? Why make a wall in virtual space? Why make the same architecture that we already know, an architecture that has come to represent spaces that simply do not welcome all of us? In the full freedom of the big big internet, why make a white cube?* I trundle slowly on, trying to find the space they've allocated to me for my work. I turn left. Forward. Wall. Right. Forward. Forward. Wall. Left. Another wall. But this time it has writing on it: wall text. Elegant. I peep my name. It says: "Residency Annex. Artist-in-Residence 2020, Phoebe Boswell."

Annex? What? In a building that does not exist, you've made for me an *annex*?

> **Annex.** Noun. A building joined to or associated with a main building, providing additional space or accommodation.
> *Verb.* Add as an extra or subordinate part.
> *Verb.* Add (territory) to one's own territory by appropriation. (*Oxford Dictionary*)
>
> *Verb.* To take control of a country, region etc., especially by force (*Oxford Learner's Dictionary*)

An annex. In a building that does not exist. I continue.

I navigate my way to the door of this place, where I'm supposed to spend the next few months, building a new world. There's a door frame. It is regular-sized. It is not the massive thing that greeted me at the front. It is not made of glass, with nature outside, abundant. It is a simple, standard door. I align myself with it awkwardly, it takes a few tries, but eventually I move across its threshold.

I find myself in a box. Tiny. A tiny cube. Small walls, and a little window at the end. Also small. The floor, unlike the rest of the museum, is made to look like wood, not marble nor shiny concrete. It has an altogether more archaic feel than the rest of the space. Archaic but also an afterthought. They annexed it on. To a building that doesn't exist. And in the limitless infinite expanse of virtual space, where walls can be made of candy floss or clouds or nothing at all, and borders can be porous or *nothing at all*, they have built me a box and said here! Here you go, make your little world—here.

That feeling of being shifted towards the outer edge of the institution, to the not-quite place, the diversity and inclusion tick-box place, the but-where-are-you-really-from place, the but-can-I-touch-your-hair place, the we're-so-glad-you're-here-with-us, please-make-us-relevant-but-you'll-never-be-in-gallery-one-with-Manet-love-so-be-proud-of-this-place place—

My immediate response is No. We're in the middle of a global pandemic, tasked with reimagining everything. Reimagining beyond capitalism, beyond the capital carceral state. Beyond walls and beyond borders. The people designing this virtual museum had all the freedom to make it anything. Limitless freedom. They were not restricted by patronage, costs, histories, legacies, bricks, geography—and yet, they created a building, appointed a director, and proceeded to place artists within constructed walls associated with constructed hierarchies. Could the limits of the imagination not stretch a little bit further than the known architecture of the museum?

Deer were wandering back into the city of London to explore, nature was replenishing because we were no longer actively squandering it, white people were posting black squares and proclaiming in frenzied delirium that Black lives do actually indeed as a matter of fact matter, and here we were, in a replica of an elitist institution that has never really made you feel safe anyway.

I missed a lot of things. I missed my friends, my loved ones. I missed touch. I hadn't been touched for weeks. I missed the casual way we used to navigate touch, breath—the ease of a hug and the freedom of breath. I did not miss the concrete walls that had now been so meticulously built into the imaginary.

I sat with my refusal for a few days. And yet I was still so keen to work with the coders. They were brilliant, clearly. Technically brilliant, this had been proven by the attention to detail they had put into making the place. The textures, the shadows, the light. My gosh, the tender sensibility of the coded shafts of light. I started to think again about what I could do in this virtual space that I cannot do in the actual. And what I realized that I could do is—I could burn it down.

I could burn it because I refuse it / You will not put me in an annex and call it hope / I could burn it for the rage that builds in our bellies whenever these spaces try to undermine us / I could burn it for all the ways this world has structured itself to fail us, to cause us harm, to commit its violences upon us / I could burn it for histories of fictive shameful hierarchy / I could burn it for modernity's insistence on unsustainable futures / I could burn it for its smugness, its inability to see itself / I could burn it so I can watch it burn and wail with all the women within me / I could burn it as a collective crematorium for all those lives lost so needlessly to Covid / It could burn in memory of Grenfell, so we will never, ever forget / It could burn like the candles in a church hall, and we could watch its flames and pray for the blessings of those departed / It could burn to give credence to the burning in my spirit / It could burn to send smoke signals to my ancestors, both past and future / It could burn because it is time to riot / It has been time / It could burn like police cars burn when we decide enough is enough / It could burn for Palestine, for all occupied territories and terrorized people / It could burn because we are lonely / and struggling now / and need to feel its warmth. It should burn for Black people, trans people, brown people, women, queer, non-binary people, the Indigenous, the disabled, the elderly, the children, the displaced and the hungry; anyone who's ever felt overlooked, marginalized, overburdened, and disavowed. Anyone who's ever pushed at the limits of the known, its binaries, that horizon line, and demanded that there *has* to be more, that this *cannot* be it, that there are whole worlds out there and within us that we are yet to know.

"Decolonization is always a violent phenomenon."
FRANTZ FANON

There's a village in Zanzibar called Makunduchi, and every year, they hold a ritual ceremony rooted in the ancient Zoroastrian religion, called Mwaka Kogwa, which translates from Swahili as "washing of the year," where the whole village comes out to air its grievances and call in the new year. In brightly colored clothes and the women singing charged, erotic songs, the community takes up banana leaves, and thwack each other with them, *thwack* for that time you took that thing from me, *thwack* for that moment you treated me with disrespect. Thwack. Thwack. An exorcism of the negative, it is energized and chaotic but communally understood. At the end of the day, the fronds are gathered and a hut is built in the center of a clearing. The mganga, the healer, enters the hut and sits down, calling for happiness and wellbeing for all. The whole village stands in a circle around him and the hut is set on fire. The healer bears its witness, bears its heat until the last moment of his endurance, and then he runs out and away from the village, in the direction from which the new year's luck will come, taking all its negative energy with him. The annex could burn like this, too. A ritual cleansing we witness together, after we've gone to war.

I tell them I have an idea, and I'm put into contact with a brilliant coder, this young kid, can't be more than 22 but looks about 12, who is as keen to burn it down as I am. Together we start discussing the anatomy of fire. Because the design of this virtual building is so accurate, so technically rigorous, we really get into the deep entrails of how to burn down a museum. What is the museum made of, from structure to fluff? We labor over its particles. And the particles of fire, what do they look like? What is the character of this fire? Is it hot heat, or is it embers? Is it fast, or is it slow? We determine that the paint would singe first, then the plaster would bubble then melt, and then the flames would get to the beams, which would snap and crackle and become brittle and splintery in the burning. Then we'd get to the insulation, so there'd be smoke. Is the smoke unctuous? Is it toxic? Does it choke? Does it poison? What are the particles of smoke? What does a smoke pixel look like, what shape does it take? Do we want the fire to start in one place—small, tiny, unnoticed, like someone has flicked a cigarette and live ash has got lost underneath a floorboard and is slowly taking revenge? Or do we want it to be more explosive, incendiary, like arson? Do we want the smoke to be thick? Yes, but not too thick—engulfing, but not so thick as to obstruct the view. Over time, we create this fire. It burns and rages and twists the annex into this mangled carcass of what once was, and then it is ash, a hole, and the flames die away. A hole in which to let the light in.

I wonder then, what next. What happens after the burning? If we burn down the institution, what happens next? Do we trust ourselves to know?

I think about all the times we are called upon by institutions to right their wrongs, to perform metaphorical burnings of their inflictions against us, and how often we become implicated, serving the purpose of freeing them from their guilt through our own time, labor, thought, care and love for ourselves and one another, how that somehow gets perversely wrapped up in the performance, in alleviating the guilt and shame of those who never choose to fully see us. So I do not stop at the burning.

We continue. The annex will burn to the ground. A slow, meticulous, majestic, ritualistic, beautiful and brutal burning. And then there is ash, and from the ash will rise a figure, a beautiful, black figure, made of ash, made of charcoal, made of embers and rage and grief and all our sorrows and all our refusals and all our humiliations and all our contributions, our successes, our conversations, and all our plotting, and all our dreaming—they will rise. And because the burning has made this hole in this at-first-impenetrable walled building, we will now be outside, in that idyllic landscape I first saw but could not reach. And they will walk down towards that emerald lake I saw outside the museum, they will reach its edge, dip their feet in, and wade out into its center, singing a primordial yet unyet heard song, guttural, knowing, and they will explode, there, in the middle of the lake.

Now, gaming technologies are cyclical, so coded narratives exist in loops. The museum will inevitably rebuild itself, then burn again, then rebuild, and burn, again and again, ad infinitum. But some things we can program to remain temporal. Over time, explosion after explosion, the sediment that lands inside the lake will begin to take shape, to accumulate and grow. Over time, an island will begin to form, in the middle of this lake, outside the museum, and made of its ash.

A new place.

A place for *us*.

So then comes the question,

What is this place? What do we need it to be?

Is it another museum, an alternative museum? Is it an archive, a living one? Does it house our stories and does it hold us when we are adrift? Is it a haven, a sanctuary, a home? Is it a home? Is it safe? What makes it safe? Does it wake us up or let us rest? Is it a spiritual place, like a church or a mosque or a synagogue? Is there an altar? Are there altars? Do we arrive one way and leave altered? How do we arrive? Is there safe passage across the water to reach it? Will there be small boats? Are we welcomed at the end of our journeys? Who is welcomed? Are there passports? Are there visas? Is it a country? Are there laws of governance? What are they and who makes them? What happens if they are broken? Is it a democracy? What does that mean? What are its belief systems? What are its politics? Is it multicultural? How does it tend to its sick? How does it bury its dead? Is it a burial ground? Is there money there? What is the currency? Or do we barter? Or is there simply enough for us all? Is the ground fertile? What can grow from this ash? Is there other life present? Other life forms? How do we cohabit? Is it even a place for us? Or is it a playground for the more-than-human? Is it a space for interspecies kinship? What if we still don't understand that? What if we just get there and ruin it because we don't know how to loosen our grip on control? What if it's not a place for us? What if it is not about us at all? What if it exists beyond our requirements for belonging and meaning, beyond our self-determinations and categorizations, and subjecthoods, and earthly existences, our enfleshment and perceptions of dominance? What if it exists beyond the poisonous methods we actively engage in that are rendering the current world unlivable? Is it a livable place? Is it a living place? Is it a loving place? Is it a truthful place? Is it a whole world or is it a fragment existing in relation to other shores? Is it a solid mass or does it break and form and have a multiplicity of meanings? Can it move? Can it move itself up or downstream? Is it affected by the tides? Is it a place where we can scream without fear of incrimination, hypocrisy, censorship, and lies?

I look back at all I've just written and how much of it falls into the trap of dreaming of something else yet constructing just another physical place, something like a nation-state, what we already know and what we know does not work. Which is wild because I've never dreamed of a nation-state. I've never felt at home in a thing called place. In Kikuyu, my mother's language, it is said that home is a river. Fluid. We need new models, new paradigms.

As a precursor to this Alchemy Lecture, I shared a brief overview of my arsoned annex and the island it creates as a thought experiment within a course titled Black Feminist Ecopoetics, created and lead by speculative writer, artist, scholar, and pleasure activist Ama Josephine Budge, to coincide with my show *A Tree Says*, an immersive work that inhabited Orleans House Gallery in Twickenham and its surrounding woodlands, and engaged the audience in an intergenerational call and response, where trees became repositories of enquiry. Ama's course explored "themes of Blackness, ecology, kinship, memory, Afrofuturism, poetics, and Black feminist worldbuilding," within the context of my show, and the audience for it was a beautiful group of mostly Black women, gathered by Black Blossoms, an organization that creates lecture series "offering a nuanced exploration of contemporary art's complex and ever-evolving landscape."

Together we tried to work through what this place is. Is it the elsewhere, the otherwise, a no place, the new place? And what became apparent, possible, was that the place, this island, this imaginary beautiful place, could in fact be exactly where we were, the communal space we were in that moment creating together, where we were giving each other space to imagine and collectively work through. Much like this space, to be honest. *Loophole of Retreat*, also. These alchemic spaces of possibility, where we can speculate, burn shit down and build it up, where we can admit that we don't know and can endeavor to know. Where we can admit that we're frightened and ask for each other's care. Where we can and will burn it all down if we have to. Where we (to quote Simone Weil) "participate in the creation of the world by decreating ourselves." "We must be rooted," not as beings but as existent things, "in the absence of place."[4]

I'm reminded of an artist talk I attended in London recently, where a young Ghanaian artist named Hassan Issah, in London for the first time to do a residency, told us of his work. First he detailed the art collectives in his hometown of Kumasi and what they do to support, cultivate, and nourish artists and artmaking practices there. He spoke passionately and at length about these hubs, then rigorously detailed the efforts of multiple artists working alongside him in his community. Following this, he took time to celebrate the skilled artisans in Kumasi who assist in the creation of his artworks. Only having defined all these rings of community and care did he then begin to talk about his own practice, framing it so entirely within the karmic circles surrounding him. I've thought so much about that talk, about the framework of knowing that without you I don't exist. That my expression is made meaningful in the existence of yours, and of the whole.

Hassan also told us what has been drummed into him by his professor, Kąrî'kąchä Seid'ou: that art is anything that is radically new, so in Kumasi, they sometimes move like they have no idea what art is at all. Art becomes bottle tops and corrugated shop fronts and dust and the accumulation of bird shit on a canvas that has been left outside on purpose. He said, "If you put a work on a wall of a gallery nothing happens to it, it doesn't even shake."

It does not even shake.

Perhaps when I say I want to burn down the annex, to dissolve the walls of white spaces and let the light in, perhaps what I mean is that I want to make art that shakes.

The Black Horizon (Do We Muse on The Sky or Remember The Sea), immersive installation, 2021.

For *Prospect.5*, I dip the central atrium of the Contemporary Art Center, NOLA, in black, creating a body of water onto which, over the course of six weeks, I inhabit with gathered images of Blackness and Black liberation. I invite fifty Black thinkers to tell me what freedom is, what freedom means to them, and how they will practice freedom today. I ask you, the heavyweights, Christina, Saidiya, Rinaldo, Maaza, but I also ask the children, Enhle, 4, Dorothy, 3½. Their—your—voices speak out from two pillars in the center of the space, at ear level. Sometimes there's overlap, sometimes clear sound, and every contribution is different. Some say freedom is everything, some say it is nothing but a delusion. A sonic bass echoing our black painted horizon plays low, from the ground, a rhythmic single note on the double bass. Up high, from the rafters of the building, a saxophone responds to the timbre of your voice with the melodies that sing like gods, prophets, ancestors, or guides.

Dwelling, **audiovisual installation, 2022.**
A black cube. You enter and find yourself immersed in this water world; water being the dichotomous site of both trauma and renewal, remembrance and futurity. I learned that 95 per cent of Black British adults cannot swim, so I booked an underwater studio and put a call out for people to bring their loved ones and help each other feel safe in the water. We set up a camera and hired a lifeguard and gave each pair a loose hour to do whatever they pleased in the pool. Fathers brought their babies, a 10-year-old boy brought his mother to teach her, there were lovers, queer kinships, siblings, each pair evoking the fragile moments of tension, fear, vulnerability, courage, and confidence required for both intimacy and learning to swim. These episodes play across floor-to-ceiling projection screens at varying speeds and loops, submerging you, accompanied by an independently looping soundscape, comprising of three scores for double bass: one for the unpredictable present. Learning to swim, set to this shifting soundscape of terror, hope, stillness, and chaos, becomes a choreography, a dance of fear, reclamation, and liberation.

Wake Work, **pencil on black paper drawings, mounted in situ at the British School at Rome, 2019.**
A series of drawings made whilst on fellowship at the British School at Rome. My live/work studio was inside this colonial institution and the coloniality choked up all the air. I made these works in tribute to three African men, Pateh Sabally, Emmanuel Chidi Namdi, and Idy Diene, who had lost their lives in violent circumstances in Italy over recent years. The

works are black pencil on black paper so they can only be seen in certain light and angles, playing with issues of presence and erasure within these traumatic stories. When Idy Diene, a Senegalese street vendor, was shot dead in broad daylight on the Vespucci Bridge in Florence, the state refused to admit that the crime was racially motivated. The Senegalese community went out onto the streets to protest, during which some municipal flowerpots were toppled over and damaged. The ensuing narrative was one of vandalism and violence, the flowerpots became the victims, and the Senegalese had to raise money to replace them. In the center of the gallery of this colonial institution, flanked by my drawings, I smashed the flowerpots from the central courtyard of the British School at Rome, stolen at midnight, without permission, in solidarity with Idy, Pateh, and Emmanuel.

Transit Terminal, in situ in my solo exhibition *Here*, at New Art Exchange, Nottingham. 2021.
Between lockdowns, we were able to finally open that show that had stood dormant mid-install from the start of the pandemic. For this new iteration, I invite diasporic people, particularly people I missed over that period, to breathe with me, to record their breath and tell me something about home. This becomes a four-channel soundscape across the gallery where the figures of Transit Terminal stand. A commingling of our breath and a meditation on home. Prior to the show opening, I extend the murmuration of drawn birds from inside the coffins onto the walls of the gallery, freeing them to fly as high and as far as they can go.

A Tree Says (In These Boughs The World Rustles), multi-phonic, multi-layered indoor and outdoor installation, 2023.

In this work, honoring our elders and the wisdom of trees, I put out a prompt on social media, asking: What are the questions you have always wanted to ask? What advice do you need right now? What do you still need to know? And gather an assortment of questions, ranging from the philosophical to the deeply personal; from the existential to the practical and everyday. In the main gallery, you are invited to sit on this forum of tree stumps, titled *The Whispers*, where each stump whispers the questions gathered. If you sit down on a stump, my voice is raised from a whisper to reveal how the initial core of questions expanded in nuance as each conversation with each elder unfolded. You are then encouraged to go outside and spend time in nature, where you'll find the answers, through the voices of our elders in the trees. I recorded interviews with twenty-eight nominated elders, each conversation rich and vulnerable, each searching for the words to articulate the truths of their long lived lives.

On The Line (The Space Between Things), site-specific wall drawing, 2018

After a life-altering event left me with a broken eye and a ruptured heart, artmaking took on new meaning; it became a lifeline, a safety mechanism, a survival strategy. When I finally began to show work again, I insisted on a slow install. Autograph in London gave me the gallery for twenty-one days prior to opening, and I masking-taped a horizon line onto the walls of the gallery. Every day I would photograph myself, naked, in whatever state I was in, and draw myself onto the line in an act of catharsis. I wanted to leave my trauma there in the gallery, and I wanted to learn how to trust again. I drew in soft willow charcoal, so soft it could disappear if you blew on it too hard, and I refused to fix it, or place a barrier, trusting that you, the audience, would treat me with care and do me no further harm.

The Lighthouse, experimental collaborative performance, 2019

A room full of women collectively reading, figuring out, in real time, how to read together from our chosen gospels, connected by a piece of mine, "Take Me To The Lighthouse," which I'd written while sick. I loved making this work, we did it twice, with an amorphous group of brilliant women who each brought so much heart and rigor to the space.

Later, I would do another version, with just my mother; her and I reading together from a transcript of her memories, reading together, learning and re-learning one another, learning how her stories fit in both of our mouths.

Mutumia, interactive installation, 2016

A salute to women who've used their bodies in protest when they haven't been permitted to use their voices. A six-channel hand-drawn animation of an army of naked women moving through different states of protest, from rage, to grief, to prayer, to shame, to sisterhood, to freedom, to resilience, back to rage, projected onto the walls of the gallery in a reverse panopticon. The floor is fitted with hidden sensors which when stepped on activate the voices of women, including a gospel choir, Kenyan writers Wambui Mwangi and Ndinda Kioko reading their feminist prose, and gathered testimony from an array of women. If the room is empty, it is silent, but if you enter the room, and acknowledge the presence of these women insisting themselves upon the white-male-dominated walls of the art gallery, you activate the voices to be heard. When the room is full, a crescendo. In each new city, I add new voices.

The first time I gathered voices was in London, and I asked women these provocations attributed to Audre Lorde's "The Transformation of Silence into Language and Action": What are the words you do not have yet? What do you need to say? What are the tyrannies you swallow day by day and attempt to make your own, until you will sicken and die of them, still in silence? If we have been socialized to respect fear more than our own need for language, ask yourself: "What's the worst that could happen if I tell this truth?"

As I gathered the voices, I transcribed and shared them between the women. I asked if they would honor each other by reading each other's answers in their own voices. Much like the collective reading experiment, I wanted them to hear their words, their fears, their dreams, and their strengths spoken by and through one another. Sami, a trans woman at the start of her transition, wrote,

> The words I do not have yet.
>
> I do not yet have the words to talk about the things that have happened to me, as if they happened to me.
>
> I do not have the words that connect me to others, without feeling like an imposter. Like I'm using another's language without truly belonging.

I do not have words that are mightier than a sword, burn hotter than fire. But I know women have these words, and I know they will come. I know mine will come.

I do have some words. Words of strength, of defiance. But yet, I do not feel immovable in my comfort with them, so I do not have these words.

I do not yet have words coming from a place of omnipotent pride, rather than an incessant and babbling stream of shame.

I do not have a lot of words I need. Not yet. But soon.

I need to say.

I need to say I love you. I love me. I love all of us. It's not my fault. Or your fault. It's never our fault. Ever.

I need to say, to be strong is not to be feared, or at least not by ourselves.

I need to say there are systems of power in place, and that they are real, and that not everything is OK. And that you know best how you exist in this world. But I need to say the world is still beautiful, even if not around us now, at least in our memories, in a place deep inside that we know is possible. I need to say we can get back there.

I need to say you are here, and I am here for some reason. Even if that reason is just to be.

I need to say I feel alive through others. And that you're important, even if I never meet you. Your joy, passion, sadness, pain, pleasure, your hopes and dreams, plans and fears, they all matter.

I need to say I feel vulnerable, and please take care of me. Of each other. I don't want to go it alone.

I need to say so much. And I'd like to say it consciously, with compassion, and only if it's necessary.

I give Sami's words to the other women in the group and she hears them read back to her, within the work.

For Every Real Word Spoken, pencil drawings with hand-drawn QR codes, 2017

I ask women to adopt Adrian Piper's stance in *Food for the Spirit* and photograph themselves, considering deeply what it means to stand in one's own presence, in one's own nakedness. I draw from these photos, long, slow, detailed pencil drawings that require time. Drawing for me is lovemaking. If I love you I will draw you and spend hours trying to learn every nook of your face. In the center of each drawing, in the apparatus each woman is holding to take their photo, I draw a QR code, which I give to the woman to own forever. They can program this code whenever to whatever they want you to listen to, watch, read, while you're looking at them. They title their own works. They converse with you, the audience, through the drawing. The drawing is alive. It is temporal, and awake.

When I show these drawings, I make a horizon for them to share in the gallery. Sami walks in and sees herself, naked and beautiful amongst these other women. Her face, I will never forget it. Perhaps something shook then. Perhaps there was a smell of burning.

I have never wanted to write a manifesto. I believe rigid things become brittle and brittle things break and I don't even really like writing artist's statements, to be honest. They keep you in that static place, they're restrictive, and they lack nuance: "this Black woman artist deals with themes of migration, identity, and gender" and once again you're in this small box with small walls and tiny windows. And you say you're making art but really you're just making the same thing on repeat to satisfy a market that has bought into what you say you're selling. I've never wanted to say anything unnecessary, that could hold me stuck in a moment, or force my hand, or constrict what and how I feel compelled to make. I've never wanted to be a world leader or make decisions that affect populations and I've never believed that I know how to fix the problems of this world—the rot of capitalism, the stench of imperialism, the decay of colonization, the perversity of white supremacy, the specter of climate catastrophe; the anti-blackness that undergirds it all. I believe these should be the decisions of the many, not of the few. But as artists, if we're lucky and brave, we make our own little worlds within our work and we invite people in and hope that these worlds might somehow ignite something that moves us towards the belief in a new place. A beautiful place. This beautiful world that we're manifesting in these pages. So, in that spirit,

> From now, into the future unknown,
> I will attempt to make art that shakes.
> I will attempt to dissolve walls and let light in.
> I will attempt to burn down that which systemically disavows, and I will grow communal speculative spaces from the ash. This burning does not need to be literal. Arson can take the form of immersive spatial takeovers, wall drawings, soundscapes, collaborations, writing that is direct and means what

it says, writing that is opaque and takes you on a journey without a destination. Work that meets you where you are, and speaks in different languages at once. Critical literacy, humor, tenderness, and care. Saying no with chest.

I will consistently reassess my own conditioning and explore all the worlds and women within me.

I will take every opportunity to heal myself.

I will create and invite people I love into spaces I believe to be safe.

We will collaborate there.

We will continue to dream of as yet unlived things.

We will do a million experiments.

I will ask questions and gather a multitude of answers.

I'll draw you and learn every nook of your face.

And I will make you chapatis and we'll eat them hot, together, straight from the pan.

Scan QR code for additional resources.

PHOEBE BOSWELL

How can we move beyond this horizon
to a place we've never been?

What is to be done, the audience clamors?
She knows they don't want an answer.

SAIDIYA HARTMAN

Crow Jane Makes a Modest Proposal

SAIDIYA HARTMAN

Crow Jane doesn't say *the sun's gonna shine in her back door some day* or lament motherless children or keen for those murdered in the streets, but she does assure us that a better day is coming, that *the arc of empire bends towards justice*, and that progress, although sometimes painful, is inevitable. As the crisis unfolds, she *humbly proposes a plan, perhaps not worthy of the attention of our esteemed audience, because it consists only of modest suggestions, a handful of her thoughts and ruminations*[1] for saving democracy, a task to which she is selflessly devoted even if it requires her to lick all the pots in hell's kitchen. Regarding the matters of racism and extermination on one hand and democracy on the other, she proffers a remedy for what can't be repaired, extols us to be patient, spins the destruction as a plan for integration and adjustment, goads us to believe what we cannot, eschewing everything *we* know about the world and imploring us to forget the long history of massacres. With brevity and forethought, she insists we pin our hopes to the project. In these terrible days of death and more death, she remains confident that this remarkable journey *we* as Americans have embarked upon will be triumphant. Imperial dreams are as unstoppable and interminable as wars without end, as manifest destiny, as *lebensraum*, as the divine mission of the settler state. An eternal empire harkens to the future.

In the fight against the threats to our existence, we are all on the same team, she coaxes, ignoring the fissures and the chasms, the divisions between citizens and animals, we stand united until we are not, until the blood bath, until democracy itself is on trial. She forgets it has always been on trial for some of us and that most of us have never experienced it. Crow Jane finds such rhetoric tedious and wearisome, crude assertions of the intellectually lazy and the identity extremists, a poor substitute for rigorous thought and incontrovertible evidence.

Optimism is never cruel, she quips, but a requirement for living. It is this presumption of good faith that makes our democracy (a republic that pits *all men* against the rest of us) exceptional and has propelled us forward since 1619. Even a word as anemic as *justice* isn't forthcoming in her ruminations on the matter of a solution to the problem of race relations and a plan for saving the empire. It is imperative to unify the divided nation (in a more old-fashioned parlance—the negro or native problem). She offers threadbare homilies about lesser evils, institutional neutrality, pragmatic actions, realist solutions, rational discourse, and the imminent dangers facing the West and menacing its borders. It goes without saying that she abhors the violence of the dispossessed. The goal repeated ad nauseum is to rekindle the "American spirit," which has been tested in recent crises. *Rights* and *reform* are words that portend a brighter future, unlike *abolition* or *reparation* or *sovereignty* or *return* which are guaranteed to stymie and derail the conversation every time. At hand is a trove of ready advice, facile solutions, and DIY instructions for the best ways of averting the disaster and surviving the predation, if only by disavowing it, even as we are knee-deep in it. Glock 43Xs, AR-15s, bunkers, citizen militias, settler confederations, red ribbons, nooses, swastikas, bones and scalps, cherished mammies, red-face mascots, and Black lawn jockeys are part of the American spirit too, and so we must learn to coexist peacefully with our differences, embrace neighbors who dream of our extermination. Her untiring optimism and dogged innocence are performatives necessary for fortifying the nation, *our democracy*, Western civilization, despite all that we have endured and the current state of emergency.

America is beautiful, exceptional, and she believes she can rescue it. At least 62 per cent of white nationalists might still be converted to pluralism or convinced that *human* rights don't threaten or depreciate the value of Man and Settler. In the aftermath of the *awful and wicked traffic* and the way of death and the trail of tears, she remains steadfast: there is an antidote for the transubstantiation of the poor white into planter oligarch[2] and state executioner, a corrective for every white citizen who internalizes the power of the police, each day reinforcing the barrier between the governable and the disposable, as if the plot against America *isn't* America, as if fungibility was a shared condition. As if the next time, the president-elect might induce the homesteaders and the supremacists to change their minds, and not storm the capitol or fire on Fort Sumter, not embrace the boogaloo and the bloodbath, and allow us to live; and after the genocide, he might stand heroically against the murder of innocents and proclaim with the necessary gravity—it's over the top. As if this is the most we could hope for or all that we should want.

Crow Jane's lecture is a composition deracinated from the field and choked with the language of the covenant, assurances of state and civility. It is reasoned, measured, never strident, to ensure the willingness to listen on the part of those who are not inclined to heed any truths dropped from *sooty* lips and who prefer to talk about the weather as we are dying, who espouse civility as the tanks roll into the city, who demand the exchange of ideas without antagonism or unrest, those for whom conquest is encounter and slavery a training school for negroes, those who are accustomed to dictating the terms of address and who possess the power to deaccession your ass in a minute. Yet, in her case, they prove willing to suspend, if only temporarily, the rules of engagement, the visceral disbelief in any worldview but their own or those hostile to their "determined chains" of meaning,[3] and cede to the native informant's predictable babble. Fortunately, she has been well educated at the most elite schools, so the master's episteme is her own. Like the quiet storm, her modest proposal is easy listening, nothing but legible speech without any discordant tones or ugly feelings; it is assimilable, digestible, delectable as good negroes are wont to be. The *so articulate* delivery extends the reassuring comfort of the familiar, mammy fascism, statecraft in Black and brownface. No hue and cry. No *fuck it*, no *burn it down*, no *complete program for disorder*, no riot, no unrepentant destruction. Just this metaphorical aptitude, this plasticity, this figurative capacity or talent for becoming whatever is required or nobody at all,[4] just the tender gift of reproductive labor *in service of* the order, the embrace of her beautiful humiliation, the betrayal of her volition, the dulcet tones of submission, the vow to wait, to keep waiting and waiting until oblivion, the propensity to endure until hardly any of us are left standing, just the appeal *father may I, master may I, man may I*, which is so much better than any pledge of allegiance.

Crow Jane, like other realists, wastes no time on what might be necessary for a state change, a new set of arrangements, but rather devotes herself to the likely, the probable, the parameters of the given. An Ivy League degree and $100,000 in student loan debt has translated the incisive critique of her forebears—same shit, different day—into her own eloquent holding pattern, a dicty expression of servitude disavowed. Though loath to admit it, in her heart of hearts, she believes the order is eternal. The admission hurts yet it is not without a small consolation—why even try to create something different, why waste the effort—the gift of pragmatism is a profound tolerance of the unlivable. The paradox is that she makes her living as a changemaker, analyzing the problem and proposing solutions for transformation, albeit incremental. In crude terms, she amends and tucks the racial order. 2020 was a watershed year. Her client list grew exponentially, as did her investment portfolio, as she penned solidarity statements for the Fortune 500, waxed poetically about the compassion of JP Morgan, Barclays, HSBC, and Lloyds and the long history of their investment in the Black community. A feature on white fascists and the love of their Black children earned her a finalist spot for the Pulitzer.

For a robust six figures, she helps institutions navigate the turbulence produced by rabble-rousers and the ungrateful, anarchists and militants, and sometimes, surprisingly, even upstanding citizens. If pushed to the wall, even decent, hard-working folks might relish the sight of a police precinct engulfed in flames (or celebrate the vision of their oppressors quaking in fear). She doesn't permit herself to consider whether her life might be better if she wasn't the Associate Director of Diversity and Inclusion or a Title IX officer, especially since most of those she takes to task for intolerance or hate speech are the university's most recent arrivals. Why can't the ethnic studies professors and DACA students just shut their mouths and do their work? Why can't they uphold the values of the university instead of attacking them? She is predisposed to this line of work—it comes naturally to her. Her father had worked his way up from an FBI informer to a big muckety-muck at the Department of Housing and Urban Development and made his reputation by eliminating more housing units in one year than had been created in the previous two decades. The demise of the Panther Party had enabled him to purchase a modest ranch-style home for his family in a less fashionable section of the Oakland Hills. It was the time before influencer mansions and media deals and multimillion-dollar antiracist centers and Black Lives Matter hedge funds. (Of course, it is small change when compared with the billions contributed to gut the judiciary, take over the state by dark money legislation, enthrone the oligarchs, restore the monarchy.) Unlike her father, Crow Jane was no judas goat, at least not at the start of her career— she really did intend to make things better, if only by being a positive role model for her race, a star of the flock, the native most fluent in the language of the Man.

Crow Jane has mastered the art of appeal and persuasion, regaling audiences with tales of American opportunity, vignettes about how she resisted drugs and pregnancy and Afropessimism, and advanced by her own merit, or enchants them with stories of her unworthiness, how she was lazy and received opportunities she didn't deserve and how it hurt her, but eventually she learned to work as hard as her white colleagues. Now (that she got hers), Crow Jane celebrates the end of affirmative action. Lavish praise is heaped on the wealthy and powerful, thanking them for their generosity and small mercies, the extracted wealth redistributed parsimoniously. She thanks the donors more than Jesus and they have opened the floodgates for her enrichment, enabling her to retire from the Manhattan Institute to create her own nonprofit, DEI Equity Partners™. Amen to that.

Her broad warm smile opens the doors. A bear hug can as easily accomplish the job when her words fail, or the environment is too hostile for speech. She can recite verbatim the chronicle of the four hundred years of transformation from captive to citizen, from tool to worker to felon, noting key dates on which our collective reputation as human was injured if not negated entirely, while balancing gracefully the promise of the oldest, greatest democracy in the world against the peril of being permanently marked as commodity and slave. Yet, in this terrible history, she discerns the working of providence.

She whets the appetites of the 1 per cent, the self-declared owners of the earth, the great soaring predators, the towering figures, the rulers of men, who still remember the stories whispered by fathers and grandfathers behind closed doors, tales about delectable flesh and rare copies of the collected works of de Sade bound in the hide of a negress, or recollect fondly their first blue movie, *Gone to the Quarters*, in which Rhett and Mammy get down. Crow Jane, outfitted in her thigh-high patent leather boots, conjuring effortlessly Patsy as negress and dominatrix until they are frenzied with rage and lust. They beg to feel her stiletto against their throat. She narrates the once upon a time from 1619 to the Voting Rights Act, explicating the origin of racism, how it was stamped from the beginning, but progress is inevitable, how merit is the best equalizer, how far we have come. Who could have anticipated the day when the name of a Black woman would be inscribed on an oil tanker? Her proposal concludes on the upbeat: as it stands, depeopled, a great nation.

To earn her keep, she learns to spin the problem in new ways and creates multiple products from how-to books to a new line of apparel. Anastasia on the new Converse and Gordon on T-shirts. The Nike Foundation hires her as a consultant when they decide to make "Refusal" a slogan for a new line of urban sportswear. Even the Fondazione Prada is doing Black Study and the Ethnological Museum has incorporated native perspectives in the wall text to contextualize their loot and disarm those demanding the return of human remains. She crafts statements of restitution. The grand pronouncements to do better and try harder mask the new idioms of predation and the same ol' routines of death.

What is to be done, the audience clamors? She knows they don't want an answer. Just words of comfort, the given clad in a new guise, and vague earnest gestures pointing toward a path forward. They leave sated. When called to appear before a congressional body assembled to address the most recent crisis, and after due consideration of the terrible events—the mass killings, the plagues, the immiseration, the war, the camps, the boats—with the obligatory gravity, she advises: The first task is to establish a commission to study the problem. The white paper, released with pomp and circumstance, offers a road map detailing the long course ahead, the slow steady road to change and what will be required of all of us as Americans and citizens. The takeaway: reform is within reach and need not be painful or jeopardize anything.

It feels good to be a role model. Young people need examples they can emulate, otherwise they risk nihilism. Melancholy historicism, as has been documented by several big data projects on the counterintuitive ratio between happiness and hunger in the Global South, is an obstacle to upward mobility and success. The morality tale about her crackhead sister, her cousin Pookie, and her drug-dealing nephew go over well with the conservatives. On special occasions, at a Juneteenth celebration or a mass funeral, she might even hum a few bars from "To Be Young, Gifted and Black" or sing off-key to "Lift Every Voice" in homage to her community.

Crow Jane has become an expert in speaking in the most efficacious manner, in a clipped brisk cadence, in a sonorous tone, with a dusky, enchanting timbre, no slipped r's or g's, but a sleek, technical presentation, with PowerPoint, statistical tables, and re(tro)gression analysis which rouses the audience, inducing self-satisfactory grins and assertions of having learned so much. Roses are thrown onto the stage and the stampede of applause lasts for several minutes. The mob loves her. But even if they booed and threw tomatoes, she would be fine. It's all part of the job. Before each public appearance she rehearses the insults likely to be hurled at her, so now even the N-word doesn't make her flinch or recoil. It would be a violation of her professional code to ever say that she was offended or respond heatedly to the most hostile question. The noisiness of rancor and hate is preferable to the cut of chilly silence and indifference. To her credit, she has never called anyone a racist as an act of self-defense. She knows these are fighting words, and the meekest will go full commando at the merest hint of the charge, so she chooses another line of approach. It is worth it if she can be of service.

The crowd loves this too—her ability to receive the slurs and the assaults, yet not fold under the pressure of attack. On one or two occasions it backfires and stokes their cruelty, and she has narrowly escaped when delight yields to wrath or the need to humiliate, when the hunger for violence overrides the safe word—democracy. Most of the time, they applaud her reasonableness, slap her on the back for being a good sport, commend her for not making a big deal of an innocuous exchange, not getting bent out of shape about a poor choice of words or hysterical about the misspelling of *niggardly* in an email from the chair, when clearly, he meant to indict the ungenerous posture of the administration, not direct a racial aspersion at the junior colleagues and recently hired adjuncts. Lessons she learned from her private life prove useful in the political arena. She never makes anyone feel bad. Even as they inflict pain she receives it as if it were desired. Her language is neutral and not charged with terms that provoke distrust and conflict. She restricts herself to "some of us" and "we," leaving the crude taxonomies of difference, the immutable badges and marks, the heritable indicators of privilege and disadvantage for the audience to decide. For a moment, they pretend to almost forget that she isn't one of them. The audience leaves sated.

Crow Jane delights in the invitation to the table. The

responsibilities of her position have been outlined clearly. In her presence, they have the same conversation they have had for the last century, but now that she is at the table, things can appear as though changed. She bridges the divide between those of us who imagine themselves as inviolable and the some of us who are disposable, the ones fixed on the losing side of the divide between life and not life. When addressing this assembly of the powerful, the donors, trustees, collectors, board of directors, she is sassy and revanchist, perfectly delivering what they like and getting them off so easily in conversation—service by the hour or the term. She appears devoted, like a martyr for America, like a Dixiecrat's wet dream, like a woman eager to get paid, like she's on the clock for the project, like declaration and allegiance are slave play, like we have all the time we need, like deliberate speed is sufficient, like she can change the world— one white mind at a time.

Crow Jane is no innocent. She is diplomat and trickster and has navigated treacherous waters. "No one group has a monopoly on truth" has rescued her from many difficult situations. After a year in her first job as the highest ranking and most visible diversity officer in the history of the corporation (a real estate company with a university attached), she has an epiphany. A yearlong search process with McKinsey & Company failed to yield one viable candidate despite the handsome fee. The truth struck her like a brick to the head, it was painful and shattering. Finding a solution to the problem was not desired. She was one of a skilled set of personnel required to provide a release valve for anger and frustration, quiet the volatility of campus life, avoid the embarrassing spectacle of raped students dragging mattresses across the stage at graduation or placards demanding divestment on alumni weekend. Her job was to assuage the hurt and ugly feelings, nurse the wounds of the privileged, endorse the validity of everyone's perspective and manage all that sensitivity. A brilliant young program officer who entered the race-and-racism industry with her had been fired after devising a plan for the return for all the value extracted from the university's stolen land and labor. She couldn't find another position, diversity and inclusion had canceled her. Rumors were rampant. Some said she was now a trader on Wall Street, others that she was a minister at a megachurch in Atlanta preaching prosperity consciousness to her struggling flock.

At Anderson Ranch, Crow Jane explains structural inequality to the millionaires. The billionaires opt out, they don't do woke. At the cocktail hour, they seek her out. Sorry I missed your lecture, but if it isn't an imposition, can you teach me to do the Stanky Leg? Outfitted in the string of pearls and Hermes scarf from her gift bag, she begins the step-by-step instruction: bend the leg and pop the knee. After her second or third glass of Château Lafite Rothschild (2019), she twerks imitating a respected prison abolitionist. The white boys are hysterical with laughter. They beg for another impersonation. Do Topsy this time.

The lecture circuit is her bread and butter. Crow Jane takes to the podium like a fish to water, like a devoted servant to the backstairs of the great house. She is no Red Peter compelled to account for his appearance before the Academy, offering a personal history of captivity and cruelty, negotiating the chasm between himself and Man. Her speech is devoted to policing the crisis and averting imminent dangers. Impaired citizenship and precarious life are no obstacle or impediment to faith in the founding fathers, a steadfastness of belief unshaken by the murder of her sister and the sentencing of her brother; true conviction is unwavering and not shaken by circumstance. No apostate on her deathbed. No yes-em to death and destruction for Crow Jane. She will continue to hold on for the last benediction.

She never despairs because she is a believer in the exceptional promise, so expounds tirelessly about what is to be done. The burning streets and the mass shootings and the state-sanctioned murders instill no doubt. She assures us, the some of us slain in the streets and murdered in our homes, that we won't have to tarry forever. We are the explicit audience of her address but beneath the demand that we do better and try harder is the hidden polemic, the words of chastisement—get your shit together because the powerful are indifferent to your complaints, your protests and slogans are unheeded. She might as well say, cast down your buckets, as she advises tolerance and fortitude, which is gold, which is better than money in the bank, which is essential to the task of creating a more perfect union. In the twenty-first century, there is no us and them. She utters the word *responsibility* eleven times and then closes with an out-of-context quote from *The Faith of the Fathers*. Wait—just long enough to get this octogenarian into office, long enough to count the ballots, long enough to quell the riots, long enough to hide the video from the body camera, long enough to extract more from the bottom, long enough to lure the nationalists and patriots, the moms for liberty and the Karens, the gun lovers and the swing voters, long enough to quiet the abolitionists, to round up the radicals and anarchists, long enough to make peaceful protest a felony, long enough to win the center right, long enough to quash all talk of antifascism, antiblackness, and Palestine, long enough to burn and ban books, long enough to subsidize the markets, engorge the rich, and canonize the venture capitalists, long enough for data points to cultivate desire, produce and direct thought, for AI to make tenured professors superfluous, long enough to exploit want, exalt and intensify the illusory autonomy of the consumer's *I* and *mine*; long enough to create new incentives for accumulating wealth and evading taxes, long enough to institute a more brutal regime of deprivation for the poor, long enough to make our cities safer, long enough to reform the police and raise their annual budgets, long enough to maim and eradicate the wretched, to watch the spectacle of our death with an orgy of tears, with sentimental hard-ons. Crow Jane condemns the looters and the rioters, the free issue, *los sin papeles*, the undocumented, the refugees, the arsonists burning the big-box retailers, the vandals defacing the proclamations and monuments, the revelers heaving Colston into the Thames. They clearly don't love liberty. When they chant, Reject the free papers, dismantle the state, she advises the governor to call in the National Guard.

The intended audience cheers, the convention hall rings with applause and shouts of praise, high-fives and awkward fist bumps. The ones clapping and heaping on the praise, the members of the assembled body, the convention, the faculty senate, the true objects of her address don't ask, *what is it*? when she is within earshot. They bite their lower lips so as not to laugh at the ungainly sight of her in the flesh-colored suit, the body bag so unkind to the darker races, they don't look askance at her large rough hands, thick wrists and broad shoulders, or joke that there is nothing petite or diminutive about her, no *negrita* or little lady, wouldn't want to drown in that hole, they chuckle and wink behind her back, man to man they concede to wanting to do her brother too, discourse on the incitement of pendulous breasts. Steatopygia or not, blond wig or not, like Jefferson they disavow the want of the very thing loathed; orangutans prevaricate in *Notes on the State of Virginia*, making even the deceiver George W. seem less so, the rapturous dalliances of predator presidents, great statesmen, and founding fathers, rapists, despoilers, rakes, lie like hell in the state of the union, the senators from the heart of the confederacy deny the monstrous intimacies of Strom Thurmond, the threnodies for dead slave girls recited with friends at the planters' club, swear on their mother's grave and the pedestal of Aryan womanhood to be loyal to the cause in the anti-miscegenation filibuster.

When they go low, she goes high, making even Uncle Tom's apotheosis seem half-hearted, sluggish. Crow Jane smiles, despite the black eye, the swollen lips, the blood filling her mouth, as she endeavors to subdue her public; yes, boys will be boys. She gives it her best effort, attempting to disarm her handlers, escape the battle royale with all her teeth and minimal bruises; exchange pleasantries with her colleagues, her allies, her neighbors, as if a bright smile or choked laughter might provide a solvent against hate, goad loathing into affection, transform negation into recognition, make analogy of antagonism. How might she rearrange their desire? Or change their mind about some of us and let just a few escape their heel? Quell their doubts by touting our accomplishments and how little of it would have been possible without the little lady who started the war, the army of teachers, the philanthropists and the

Society to Protect and Care for the Darker Races? She rewrites the history of slavery and its afterlives as a story of interracial cooperation and friendship, insisting the slaves have no heirs. This abject groveling doesn't shield her from indifference or prevent her from enmity or the blunt force of contempt and derision. A pit of doubt opens in her solar plexus. Has she been wrong about everything? In a moment of panic before the sea of Anglo-Saxon faces, she wants to retract everything. A voice in her head pleads, *get me out of this now?* But how? She could bolt from the podium, however there is nowhere to run and hide, she wouldn't get far before her hosts blocked the path and asked, *what the hell are you doing?* They didn't pay her for this nonsense. She counts to ten and catches her breath, composes herself, and proceeds, she is exhausted before she opens her mouth, humbled with gratitude, earnest and brimming with shame. Incorporated by the structure, puffed up with the little power they have deigned to give or concede, she laughs at herself, as she ventriloquizes the language of state and empire. She laughs exquisitely, she goes for the language of the mountaintop when they reach for the tiki torches, she reiterates the pledge: *I am not trying to reconstruct anything.*

When Crow Jane explains the scheme, the plan for our obliteration sounds like a promise to do right by us, like a proclamation of *eventually, in due time, except as punishment for crime*. She has been listening to them for so long that she thinks as they do, rationalizing death, evenly apportioning blame, imploring us to do better, berating the slags, the unhoused and impoverished for not prospering, explaining away each tragedy until the last of us disappears. A quiet extinction, like bees and whales and insects and polar bears. A slow death. It is a tragedy, Crow Jane concedes, but we can't save everyone. We too are culpable. Aren't we the agent and executioner? Why love a hood rat, why hook up with a drug dealer? We are at fault, she contends, because of who we love and how we live. Guilty because the decent reside with the criminal. The parallel societies must be extirpated. Crow Jane cautions us to be reasonable, pleads with us not to rush out, not to burn, loot, and destroy. Van Jones cries on the Jumbotron and asks us to weigh it carefully—the legal facts of the new regime vs. our narrative. To make the choice—the state or our sister? When Crow Jane concludes her chronicle, the audience is attentive, but silent, uncertain whether to laugh or hiss.

SAIDIYA HARTMAN

What is to be done, the audience clamors?
She knows they don't want an answer.

The subjunctive is the smuggler who crosses the
border of the future bearing unknown cargo.

CRISTINA RIVERA GARZA

Subjunctive:

A Manifesto About Language, Territory, and the Yet to Come

CRISTINA RIVERA GARZA

> inside us, the past, present, and future
> happening at once, we are found this way,
> together, a people spliced by empire
> GIOVANNAI ROSA

1: A Site of Irruption

"El hubiera no existe," claims a famous Mexican adage, referring to the past tense imperfect, also known as the past tense pluperfect, of the subjunctive. But Spanish-speakers are so prone to employing the subjunctive—a grammatical mood that refers to hypothetical situations, also useful in expressing wishes, hopes, suggestions, or even commands—that the opposite could be argued just as forcefully: the subjunctive, in its multiple conjugations, is the only verbal mood that exists! The *hubiera* signals what is not there, but once was, powerful and alive in the imagination. It points out an empty space, but one pregnant with possibility. This could have happened, is what the *hubiera* means, when it did not end up happening. I could have done it, but didn't, is also implied in a regretful mode. If I were. I insist she be. I wish or wished. Ojalá que. In either case, a reality was conceived, fancied, conjured up. In the world of the subjunctive everything remains alive, if only tentatively. As if on the brink.

It is an entrance.

First image: Some birds can fly nonstop, remaining airborne for weeks and even months without food or rest. The bar-tailed godwits migrate thousands of miles from Alaska to Tasmania without ever landing, and the common swifts spend most of their lives in the air, catching insects, drinking, and sleeping while on the wing. This vigorous engagement with air, this uninterrupted flight that might as well resemble pure suspense in the human eye, gives us the first image of the subjunctive.

In the early years of the twentieth century, my paternal grandparents, José María Rivera Doñez and María Asunción Vásquez, left their native San Luis Potosí and walked all the way up to the coal mining towns of northern Coahuila, close to the US-Mexico border, hoping to improve their lot in life. Drought and precariousness had pushed them north, and hope and stubbornness, something akin to faith, might have kept them going. Having lost a child and lacking any possessions but what they were wearing or carrying with them, I doubt they thought much of the future during those tiring journeys. "Where do you see yourself in five years" might have sounded like an impolite, if not openly offensive, question. But I do imagine them pausing every now and then, long enough to take in the rough landscape and ponder what was in store for them. *Ojalá que nos vaya bien esta vez*, they could have whispered into each other's ears, wishing for a better outcome this time. Their voices low, so as to not tempt fate. He might have refrained from saying "when I find a job," opting instead for the more cautious "if I were to find a job," hinting at the adversity they faced as Indigenous migrants in a perennially hostile land. *Quizá ese sea nuestro destino*, she could have pointed out as they came near the outskirts of a hacienda, secretly wishing they could rest, if only for a night. Did that scattered village become their destiny? Perhaps not. *Hubiera sido bueno quedarnos ahí.* They both knew that, when the future offered them so little, it was better not to poke at it. It was better to draw near it with tact, delicately, not hoping for much. The subjunctive of a language they spoke with a hint of an accent—the echo of a tongue they had concealed or lost—allowed them to express desire and dread simultaneously, a mix that carved a tight, airless chamber into their chests. They could breathe, albeit with difficulty: hoping for the best while readying themselves for the worst. When Walter Benjamin's angel strove to untangle her wings from the storm of the future, looking back insistently as the gusts of air propelled her forward, she might have made out my grandparents' shadows down below as they trudged through the scrubland of northern Mexico. Their stride, as steadfast as it was winding.

First thesis: The subjunctive lays the groundwork for the irruption.

Circa 1905, they arrived in Nueva Rosita, a mining town in the state of Coahuila, where they lost a second son they had named Amado, the loved one. They resided there for a while, but did not settle down, wandering instead from mining town to mining town until they found work above ground in a hacienda near Zaragoza, a border village surrounded by eight springs. Did they look into the future's eyes ready to issue a declaration about their role in what was to come? Did they have a plan and follow that plan as faithfully as they could? I doubt it. They knew what the future held for them—centuries of dispossession and displacement had left long-lasting imprints on bodies, minds, and spirit—so they harbored little curiosity and less patience for the statements of fact that plowed through the yet to come with verbs in the indicative. Instead, they daydreamed, they mused, they concocted stories in that tentative, hypothetical mode they employed when trying to break away from the wrath of the future.

I bet what interested them about that future they knew by heart was precisely what they were unable to fathom. The unimaginable, that's what they were after. Not the interrogation of nor even the contestation against this future, but what lingered in ecstatic suspension, like a bird flying uninterruptedly for months, before it could even be conceived and much less pronounced. Not this future, but another tense altogether—the story of which they had to safeguard tenderly, concealing it even from themselves. Slivers of this story leaked out at times as they spoke about deeply held wishes, wild hopes, desires too delirious to be admitted. Wishful thinking.

Second thesis: The subjunctive is the shortcut to the unimaginable.

Third thesis: The subjunctive is the vanishing point of the future.

Did José María and María Asunción ever imagine a granddaughter of theirs, bent over a desk, writing their migrant story almost a century later? Perhaps. Perhaps not. If I were them, I might not have imagined something like this, but I might have secretly wished for it, almost in disbelief, betraying all common sense. If I had been them, I would have wished this story to be shared, but in as nuanced and faltering a way, in as tense and labored a manner, as life is or could become at times. If I were them, I would not have harbored a want, but a desire flickering deep within language, which is to say deep in the flesh, unconfessed.

Fourth thesis: The subjunctive does not express wishes, but secrets.

Fifth thesis: The subjunctive is the smuggler who crosses the border of the future bearing unknown cargo.

2: If I Burned the World Around Me Until It Shone Beautiful and Brown

"If I were a woman," writes Ashley M. Jones, Alabama's first Black poet laureate, in a poem that takes readers to a phantasmagorical summer vacation on the shores of the subjunctive—a mood that, in English, uses the bare form of a verb (the infinitive without the particle "to") in a finite, tenseless clause, and employs the verb "were" to establish the hypothetical. Unlike Spanish-speakers, who regularly employ as many as six subjunctive conjugations on any given day, English-speakers lack a specific verb form to refer to imaginary or unreal situations, events contrary to fact. This has not prevented Ashley M. Jones from bringing into play the clauses and phrases that conform the subjunctive in English to interrogate the gender and racial injuries of a language that all too often conceals or disguises them. Weaving together a series of conditional clauses ("If I were a wanted woman," "If I knew," "If I were made of sun") that follow a cause-and-effect format from which the effect has been removed, Ashley Jones produces a rarefied atmosphere full of uneasy uncertainties. What would happen if the poetic voice were a woman? If she were on the beach? If her heart were held wrong? If she were pain? In withholding the effect of these conditions phrased as if imaginary, the poem not only questions the thin line that divides what is real from what's not, but also implicates the readers' ethical imagination.

Identities, gendered and otherwise, grow increasingly blurred, or alterable, in a poetic territory gradually becoming pure political alchemy: "If I were on a beach with that man—if, this time, that man dissolved into sand. If the sand became hot under my feet but my feet were gold. If a woman were made of sun. If I were made of sun. If I burned the world around me until it shone beautiful and brown. If this burning was called healing. If the healing made light." The mutation from man into sand allows for the dissolution of the male, while the female body hardens from flesh into gold, and from gold into a piece of the sun, only to turn eventually into powerful sunlight, strategically mixing the human and the non-human—and setting them ablaze.

Unleashed by the power of the hypothetical, this frenetic succession of transmutations offers no respite and no conclusion as the malaise turns into full, if indirect, rage. What if I were made of sun? What if I were to burn the world around me until it shone beautiful and brown? This shifting arrangement and rearrangement of dissimilar materials, where the organic and the inorganic, the inert and the reactive, readily exchange places, corresponds to a geological milieu that is already a "mesh of overlapping, divergent, interconnected and dispersed systems" and a temporality (and duration) that includes the notion of deep time.

Claire Colebrook has called this milieu a climate, which, "derived from concepts of surface and habitation," cannot be reduced to "[the] terrain upon which we find ourselves, but something that binds us to *this time* on the earth, with its own depletions and limits." Climate here is both meteorological and sociocultural: a way of living and theorizing and, therefore, enunciating. Mexican author José Revueltas would have described it as a belonging, a term he used to refer to the material *ubicación* (location) of bodies on the surface of an always already shared earth. Rather than a mere description, belonging constituted in his view a "burning question," one able to address the uneven, and therefore conflicting, connections between human and non-human bodies, and their mutual, if shifting, entanglements. Moreover, a belonging signaled not only a relationship with or among present bodies, but also, perhaps fundamentally, with or among absent ones. Interrogating this absence—asking, for example, who or what lay here where I now place my feet—allowed him to radically question the notion of the world as a *tabula rasa*, bringing up the ethical nature of our material and spiritual enmeshments. Climate change, which Colebrook defines as a "radical alteration of knowledge and affect," "a mutation of cognitive, political, disciplinary, media and social climates," may as well be, in José Revueltas's terms, a radical de-belonging.

Sixth thesis: The subjunctive is not only a grammatical mood but also the constitutive materiality of a climate.

The desire to burn and the act of burning follow each other closely in Ashley M. Jones's poem, setting off destruction but also healing. What the subjunctive lacks in concrete language or positive calls for action or forward movement, it produces, and in abundance, in terms of potency. *Transfiguration* is the other name of this house. *Dismantling*, what ensues. But the undoing of this world, described here as "beautiful and brown," escapes both the violent rhetoric of white-nationalist accelerationism as well as the apocalypse habit, the tragic narrative of the Anthropocene, keen on mourning the end of the White Man, shedding a new golden light on the unexpected.

3: Fog Shoes

In 1980, the historian E. Bradford Burns published *The Poverty of Progress*, a slim volume in which he examines the innumerable popular struggles that impacted, and in some cases thwarted, modernizing efforts throughout Latin America during the nineteenth century. Instead of a smooth ascending line toward nationhood and modernity, this sobering account of revolts, insurrections, riots, and revolutions offered a complex picture of a region that, however diverse, keenly resisted the incursions of capitalism and its extractive enterprises with every strategy imaginable. From armed revolts to religion-based mobilizations, from fleeing into the mountains to forming unions, peoples from Latin America fought against state-making projects that either excluded them, relegating them to the outskirts of cities and the countryside, or sought to incorporate them in subservient positions as cheap labor or political pawns. Progress, a concept ardently professed by Latin American elites into the present, meant the break-up of traditional communities, land dispossession, various forms of forced labor, repression, incarceration, the lack of material and psychological welfare, and, ultimately, death. Progress meant precarity. For many in Latin America, and elsewhere, precarity has been a synonym of progress, not its opposite. Perhaps this is the reason why the producers of *Elysium*, a dystopian sci-fi movie set in the year 2154, chose Iztapalapa, a poor neighborhood in Mexico City, as the representation of a dilapidated earth. The future has always been in the past. The Aymara people, well-versed in anti-colonial strife in the highlands of the Andes, had it right when they pictured the future as a weight on the shoulders of akapacha, the here-and-now of history, while beholding the past as it lingered ahead of them in a radically different mapping of time.

Second image: Away from family and community, desperately searching for a land they could call their own, José María and María Asunción trail across Aridoamerica at steady stride. To the birds that spend most of their lives in the air, sleeping and mating on the wing, my grandparents are but a series of shuffling shadows on the surface of the earth. There are many of them all of a sudden, men and women who travel lightly and move in haste, like spores. Expelled. Homeless. Hopeful, perhaps. The birds cannot make out their clenched jaws from afar, their tight fists. In the distance, birds cannot fathom the entanglements my grandparents welcome or are forced into, many unimagined in the past. Examples vary. In the cave where they find momentary solace one night, they cohabitate, unbeknownst to them, with a black bear. They offer their arms, literally extending their upper limbs toward bosses or *mayordomos*, as they draw close to ranchos or mining towns, trying to sell their labor force. They talk to others like them, wandering laborers deprived of land and means of production, trying to figure out what to do or where to go next. They meander, ponder, roam; they risk. They live in the subjunctive. They've been expelled, and they have yet to find a home.

Seventh thesis: The future is the longest dead end.

Accepting the material condition of precarity is central to the feminist counter-apocalypse narrative offered by Joanna Zylinska in *The End of Man*, a book she published in 2018. Looking for a radical alternative to heavily gendered and racialized Anthropocene narratives keen on the end of the White Man, Zylinska first underscores the always already relational nature of human and non-human entanglements. In tune with Italian activist Bifo, who is also suspicious of the neoliberal fairy tale of eternal prosperity, especially for the working class, Zylinska conceives of the feminist counter-apocalyptic framework as one able to create "a space for an ethical opening to the precarious lives and bodies of human and nonhuman others—including the male bodies and minds that have been discarded in the downsizing process of disruptive semiocapitalism. In doing so, it promises liberation from the form of subjectivity that is pinned to a competitive, overachieving, and overreaching masculinity. It also prompts us all to ask: if unbridled progress is no longer an option, what kinds of coexistences and collaborations do we want to create in its aftermath?"

Always guarded against concepts and practices of development, modernity, and statehood, Mesoamerican Indigenous communities have historically faced the yet to come based on a relationship of "mutual possession" with the earth. As Floriberto Díaz discusses in *Escrito: Comunalidad, energía viva del pensamiento mixe*, the state of belonging to a community in the Oaxacan highlands has relied, and relies to this day, on the capacity to produce and reproduce their material reality. Central to this arrangement are forms of labor and governance that may appear as sci-fi chimeras to contemporary observers unable to visualize a future without capitalism or the state: tequio, a type of obligatory and free labor that every member offers to the rest of the community on a rotational basis, as well as direct democracy through assembly debate. Comunalidad, the name of this alternative to state management of the commons, has allowed the Mixe and other peoples from Mesoamerica to survive five hundred years, and counting.

In Mixe, the subjunctive is called a *modo irrealis*.

Demographically speaking, Mexico was an Indigenous country at the onset of the revolution for independence in 1810, but attacks on communal property and Indigenous ways of life took apart entire communities during the nineteenth century. Those who found themselves without or outside of their *belonging* were forced to roam the countryside. Chance encounters transform us, Anna Tsing argued as she linked her definition of precarity to indeterminacy in *The Mushroom at the End of the World*. Unable to rely on a stable community or status quo, matsutake pickers, as many precarious workers before and after them, faced a world devoid of teleology with strategically designed collaborations that frequently entailed life-or-death decisions. Defined by Tsing as "a condition of being vulnerable to others," precarity forces the many to live "life without the promise of stability." My grandparents managed to enter into a series of coexistences, however fragile and short-lived, as they became migrant laborers in the north of Mexico, in regions close to the United States, transforming themselves into full fronterizos.

Third image: The faces of the cotton pickers are blurry on the photographs—the once-glossy paper now scratched, corners badly bent, signaling the passage of time. Or indifference, perhaps. Neglect. Busyness. But pay attention, take off your glasses and bring the pictures closer to your eyes. Breathe on them, and then breathe with them. In tandem. Their faces emerge now from the haze, upright and cheerful, their eyes locked on yours. What did you expect? They ask. Caught by surprise, a hand lingers momentarily in the air, halfway to the cotton bud, while a face, turned toward the camera, opens into a solar grin. Shirtless men standing on piles of cotton glance down at you, who observe from the perspective of the photographer on the ground. Women wearing hats and aprons laugh and frown at the camera, undecided between posing or carrying on with the pizca, undistracted. Stop it, they'd say, feigning shyness. Enough. Teenagers take a break from their parents, and kids, interlacing arms, attempt a pose, focused and mischievous, giggling at the flash. Bring the picture close to your ears now and feel the mad galloping heartbeat that unknots the echo of their laughter. If birds flew into the perimeter of the scene, announcing the end of summer, the unplanned nature of time. If the flight, uninterrupted, were but a tangent. If the kids of those kids were looking into themselves, spliced by empire.

Having survived the 1910 Mexican Revolution, the Rivera grandparents paid close attention to the agrarian reform efforts of the new regimes and, with them, set out to expand the desert threshold through social and agricultural experiments centered on cotton. They formed sporadic communities—shape-shifting arrangements with the state, other wandering laborers, and most fundamentally with cotton, a crop of relevance in the international market that led, however fleetingly in northern Mexico, to social mobility and a sense of autonomy landless peasants had seldom experienced in the past. By the late 1920s they had settled briefly on lands near Monterrey, Nuevo León, to start a new life as cotton pickers around the Don Martín. When infrastructural failure brought this first experience to an abrupt end, they followed their instincts and fled once again, this time on wagons along with hundreds of other families, still looking for the piece of land for which they did not obtain legal titles until 1947, in the neighboring state of Tamaulipas, with documents that featured misspelled last names. They made decisions on short notice, adapting quickly, perhaps even gracefully, to the sway of things. They placed bets and, for the moment, a moment shaped by indeterminacy, they won. The prize was survival. It only took twenty more years, however, for export monoculture to deplete the soil and expel both cotton and cotton-working communities from the area, starting a new cycle of ecological degradation and economic instability.

Eighth thesis: The subjunctive is the grammatical mood of precarity.

A good portion of the world's population has approached what is yet to come only tentatively, wearing fog shoes. More a hesitation than a plan. More a desire, perceived by others as madness, than a want. While the future is a declaration of a fact, a conjugation under the umbrella of the indicative mood, the subjunctive meanders, ponders, tempts, always looking sideways. There, where the future tense plows through, having chosen a path among many, decisively activating one option among the millions that lay dormant within its purview, the subjunctive embraces them all, keeping them alive. Like Benjamin's destructive character, the subjunctive stands permanently at the crossroads, for it sees—it must see—ways everywhere.

4: On the Actual Ground

[In conversation with visual artist Saúl Hernández-Vargas and his video *Third Lunar Limb*, screening at Aurora Picture Show, East End, Houston, September 29, 2023]

First, the war. On February 2, 1848, Mexico and the United States signed a peace agreement known as the Treaty of Guadalupe Hidalgo, with forty thousand dead people as witnesses. In the pursuit of *paz* (peace, in Spanish), a concept intrinsically linked to two other telling words, *pago* (payment) and *pacto* (agreement), Mexico was forced to cede 55 per cent of its territory, which encompassed the states of Alta California,

New Mexico, and portions of Sonora, Coahuila, and Tamaulipas. Diplomats from both nations delineated this territorial concession, or rather its severance, using the term *frontera* (border, in Spanish), which conveys a facade, that is, a front, and the word *lindero* (boundary), rooted in the Latin *linde*, also suggesting a threshold which establishes a radical relationship with space (*limen*), and consequently couples it to the sublime (*sublimus*). The border described in the Guadalupe Hidalgo treaty denoted back then, as it does now, a threshold that presented as a sublime entity that exceeds our senses. And it does, but not without complexities and ambiguities.

Fourth image: *Regulus calendula*—this is the name that enters the surveys conducted shortly after the signing of the Treaty of Guadalupe. Serene, indifferent perhaps, as they delicately feed on flowers and tender shoots, the birds surround the group of surveyors, engineers, and soldiers who pause, mounted on horseback, to contemplate the landscape covered in low bushes. Mesquites. Chamizo flowers. Eventually, other plants will be cataloged meticulously in the scientific records, turning the territory into a transparent, understandable, and colonizable entity. Meanwhile, the men dismount, holding axes and knives, compasses and theodolites. Satisfied and free, without burdens of any kind, the birds take to the skies. As if weightless.

Article V of the Treaty of Guadalupe laid the foundation for surveyors and engineers to establish the borderline with "due precision" in subsequent years. Although "to establish" may not be the right verb for the job; perhaps "to mark," "to delineate," "to outline" would be more fitting, or "to draw," as visual artist Saúl Hernández-Vargas argues. Aided by pencils or pen and ink, brushes or paint, drawing involves the sketching by means of lines. To draw is to trace bodies or ideas on a surface, usually paper or other two-dimensional materials. Mostly concerned with structure, shape, or value, drawing not only produces emotions but also, and especially when attempted on the surface of the earth, wounds of long-lasting political significance.

Ninth thesis: The US-Mexico boundary is a line.

Enigmatic at times, but vague and contradictory above all, Article V of the Treaty of Guadalupe Hidalgo provides the first description of the US-Mexico border as it would come to be known in the future: a line 3152 kilometers long that begins at the southernmost point, on the crossroads between the cities of Tijuana and San Diego, and extends itself into southern New Mexico. Beyond that juncture, the line deviates from its straight course, yielding to the contours of the Rio Bravo, or Rio Grande, as it is called in the United States, until it reaches the perennially Siamese cities of Matamoros and Brownsville, to finally flow into the Gulf of Mexico.

The taming of rivers has been central to state-making efforts worldwide. As James Scott argues in *Against the Grain*, emerging proto-states treated swamps, marshes, fens, and wetlands as untamed nature and, therefore, as trackless waste, dangerous to health and safety. They resented the malleability of mud and replaced it with its purer constituents, land and water. Emerging extractive economies depended on the draining of marshes, so they could become orderly grain fields and villages. In 1848, with the drafting of Article V of the Treaty of

Guadalupe Hidalgo, diplomats and soldiers endeavored to tame a river, setting a quivering borderline alongside it, right in the middle of its course. But can you turn water into cartilage, barbed wire, metal fringe, stone? If the riverbed kept on wandering, albeit millimetrically, over time. If the mud became slippery under my feet, but my feet were feather. If I were pure plumage in midair. If I was air. If the thousand eyes of the air glanced at a motionless wall, crossing through it. Above it. If this crossing were called remembrance. If remembrance of the yet to come were now.

Article V of the Guadalupe Hidalgo Treaty mandated the division of a substantial portion of the territory with scant regard for both the surface of the earth and the labor of the workers. Those issuing orders from well-lit offices paid no heed to whether the land was shrouded in thickets and underbrush, whether the desert proved as harsh as settlers' later accounts alleged it to be, whether the scarcity of water claimed many lives. Exhausted, perhaps annoyed, reading in the flickering glow of an alcohol lamp at one of his work encampments, Mexican surveyor José Salazar Ylarregui wrote: "on paper, drawing a line with a ruler and a pencil is easily done, but on the actual ground, it's an entirely different matter."

If it were an entirely different matter.

On the actual ground.

Drawing is a political art of deadly consequences. Marking the land and wounding the land are, at times, one and the same. As featured in Article V, the line drawn between Mexico and the United States constitutes a straight and geometric device of modernist aspirations, alien to the territory. Among multiple injustices, the line has embodied the inability of the nation-state to engage with human and non-human beings beyond the paradigm of profit. Paradoxical, the borderline that cuts and divides also links and bonds—a painful reminder of our coexistence. While it has historically separated communities and families, fracturing and alienating the territory, the line can only be understood as a relationship.

Tenth thesis: If the border is primarily a line, then it is possible, if not urgent, to undraw it. Even, or especially, on the actual ground.

Many years before Mexico became an independent nation on September 16, 1821, the border ratified by the Spanish crown and the United States in 1795 only existed in documents such as the Treaty of San Lorenzo. In Article II, brief and written with an urgency born of the conflicts of the time, the treaty marks the border, producing it: "The Southern boundary . . . shall be designated by a line beginning on the River Mississippi at the Northernmost part of the thirty-first degree of latitude North of the Equator, which from thence shall be drawn due East to the middle of the River Apalachicola or Catahouche, thence along the middle thereof to its junction with the Flint, thence straight to the head of St Mary's River, and thence down the middle thereof to the Atlantic Ocean." Five decades later, a border conceived in a diplomatic agreement transitioned into a tangible international boundary. Over time, it became a territory clearly delineated by a series of boundary markers—signs of dispossession and precarity for existing communities. Ultimately, for the United States, this territory evolved into a space regulated and governed by distinct laws and foundational myths, encompassing the Old

West, Manifest Destiny, and the prominence of individualism and freedom of choice. To render this territory comprehensible, the United States utilized proto-ethnographic accounts from border boundary commissions and an array of mapping projects funded locally and federally. The outcome was a demarcation. Over time, people came from one end to the other. They built houses. They witnessed the construction of the first railroad. They opened businesses. They plundered and thrived.

Eleventh thesis: Undrawing a line marked on the surface of the earth cannot be done in isolation. It is a communal task, a collective breath, a pretext to share the air with others.

Just as documents are reactivated when read, when touched by hands and eyes, territories often display their sediments, and the scars that keep them together, when explored and paid attention to. Territories offer each crushed, depleted, interrupted future as guidance for an alternative future. In this vein, Saúl Hernández-Vargas has suggested that because there are prior images of the US-Mexico border, such as the one depicted in the Treaty of San Lorenzo, it is not only possible but imperative to reimagine it elsewhere. Or nowhere else. If this line were mud, fusing land and water, slippery under my feet. If my feet were feather. If I were plumage and flesh, sleeping and feeding on the wing. If the thousand eyes of air made out the space where there once was a wall. If this absence were justice. If justice was now.

Twelfth thesis: On the path of radical imagination, imagining and unimagining guide our steps.

Fifth image: In a 2022 video installation, French visual artist and activist Laure Prouvost featured the slow transformation of human arms into tentacles, into wings, as she called for the end of all borders—or front tears, as stated by the protest signs she held while participating in demonstrations for human and other-than-human rights. Her augmented reality piece for CIRCA—a giant colorful octopus wrapped around the Anteros statue in London—evoked the embeddedness of migration routes of all species on Planet Earth. Could we be octopus swimming across oceans, no papers or suffering required? Could we be birds who belong to no nation?

5: Languages Don't Die, They Are Killed

In the late seventies, French experimental writer Georges Perec embarked on a visit to Ellis Island to craft a script for the film *Récits d'Ellis Island* by Robert Bober. The ultimate site of exile, simultaneously a non-place and a nowhere, where "frazzled bureaucrats baptized Americans in droves," Perec's Ellis Island remained, however, "a memory potentially our own . . . a probable autobiography." Just as Saturn devoured his offspring, Ellis Island received the poor and the dispossessed, offering them a new life, a future, in exchange for their past and their histories, their names, their languages. Perec fixated on the "closure, or severance, or cleavage" of that moment, which he sensed deep down as his own, estranged from himself, different from his own people. Where others might have seen landmarks or relics in the "chaotic assemblage of things" left in a place that had been plundered more than once, he only perceived "something shapeless, on the outer edge of what is sayable." As for the feeling that he was made up of the memories he was not allowed to learn, a bewildered Perec suddenly admitted: "I don't speak the language my parents spoke."

In a world of radically decreasing linguistic diversity, where states fight on a daily basis and to the death against languages not their own, Perec's acknowledgment vividly speaks of the plight of migrants everywhere and to Indigenous languages above all.

What does it mean to not speak the language spoken by one's parents and ancestors?

How are languages lost? How are they made and unmade?

It is land, water, and trees that nourish our languages, Mixe linguist and language activist Yásnaya Elena Aguilar asserted when addressing Mexico's House of Representatives at the Legislative Palace of San Lázaro on February 26, 2019, thus linking the survival of both language and the earth in a single stroke, turning them into a common material and cognitive territory. Languages don't die, they are systematically, steadily, brutally killed. A language dies out when its practitioners are displaced from their land, robbed of their water resources, and dispossessed of their forests. A language dies out when its practitioners are beaten, discriminated against, and assassinated on a regular basis. Hunger, repression, racism, and structural inequality slaughter both languages and the bodies of those who utter them. "Not only our lives and struggles are interconnected by histories of imperialism, colonialism, and militarism, and by increasing economic interdependence," similarly argues poet and Korean-English translator Don Mee Choi. "But our languages are also interconnected." Defending a language and defending a territory are one and the same. Linguistic rights are human rights.

Thirteenth thesis: Let us say, with Yásnaya Aguilar, that greater political autonomy for Indigenous Peoples translates into greater linguistic diversity for all.

Indigenous languages around the world face a powerful common enemy: the monolingual wrath of a state that conceives of languages other than its own as mortal threats. Stateless languages, not minority but minoritized languages, are subject to discrimination by the institutions of a nation-state. Whether because they are excluded from the administration, education, and media of a country or because of the denial of resources to promote their development, or even their usage, within specific speech communities, these languages become endangered species over time. One example among many: in 1820, at the dawn of Mexican Independence, about 70 per cent of the population spoke an Indigenous language. It has taken the modern Mexican state about a century to forcibly silence these languages, now spoken by only 6.1 per cent of Mexicans.

The United States is the second-largest Spanish-speaking country in the world, with an estimated sixty million Spanish-speakers—eleven million of them counting as bilingual Spanish/English-speakers. A language backed by the state and its military across vast regions of Latin America, Spanish turns into a stateless language on the other side of the border, sharing a condition akin to Indigenous languages throughout the world. Bilingual writer and Chicana activist Gloria Anzaldúa defined the series of structural and everyday forms of violence against Spanish as linguistic terrorism. In her native Texas, where she was born practically on the US-Mexico border, near the cotton fields that allowed for the survival of my grandparents, the intermingling of Spanish and English gave way to a mercurial blend of at least seven different wild tongues: from Castilian Spanish to mainstream English, with standard Mexican Spanish, northern Mexican Spanish, Chicano Spanish (with variations across Texas, New Mexico, Arizona, and California), Tex-Mex, and pachuco (also known as caló) in between. Anzaldúa spoke all of them throughout her life and, in writing *Borderlands/La Frontera: The New Mestiza*, the groundbreaking work that redefined our relationship to the US-Mexico borderlands, she employed not only a range of literary genres, from non-fiction to poetry, but also a supple mixture of Spanglish that startled the US academic world. Tellingly, she received her Ph.D. from University of California Santa Cruz only posthumously.

Like many English-Spanish bilingual children, Anzaldúa experienced ridicule and physical punishment for speaking a language other than English while growing up. Her schooling and bureaucratic relationship to the state were conducted solely in English. Parents concerned with the future well-being of their children encouraged the early adoption of English. But killing Spanish took on a new meaning in places such as Marfa, in the high desert of the Trans-Pecos of Texas, between the Davis Mountains and Big Bend National Park when, in the fall of 1954, teachers at the segregated Blackwell Elementary School organized a highly ritualized burial of Spanish, the native tongue of the great majority of the students. Children were asked to write the words "I will not speak Spanish" on scraps of paper, place them inside a cigar box, and stand beneath the US flag while a teacher proceeded to bury Spanish and declare it dead. Afterwards, children caught speaking Spanish were escorted to the principal's office and received an exemplary punishment: at least three heavy paddle blows. Bruises vanished before long, but memories of this institutionalized form of violence remain painfully alive in Marfa even today, where some Blackwell graduates have come together to convert the elementary school into a national historic site.

Only sixty-three years after Blackwell Elementary closed its doors, the University of Houston launched the first Ph.D. program in creative writing in Spanish in the United States in 2017, the year the White House removed Spanish from its official web page. MFA programs at UT El Paso, the University of Iowa, and New York University have helped prove that, while Spanish is proudly a language of labor, it is also a language of reflection and creativity, critical thinking and practice.

Fourteenth thesis: One, two, three, four! Creative writing programs in Spanish everywhere and elsewhere!

Sixth image: Card 19 of the Mexican lotería features a white heron standing in shallow water, her long neck stretching downward as a small red fish lies inert in her pointed beak. When she bends her limbs as if crouching and quickly leaps into the air, she is ready to take flight, extricating herself from the card. Slow wingbeats rip the Houston sky—the neck held back against the body, the delicate legs trailing beyond the tail. Her broad wings. The feathers. *Mira nada más, Cristino*, my maternal grandmother could have said as she pointed up. Does the heron look back at them right there and then, curious about this couple who, having crossed the US-Mexico border as children, have continued to labor in the ranches and cities of Texas? Does she pity them, these earthbound humans who lack her ability to cross borders without so much as a blink? Emilia Bermea Arizpe and Cristino Garza Peña are prone to correct each other over the years: it is no longer the Rio Bravo but the Rio Grande, they say. It is not algodón, but cotton, the crop that will ultimately become the key for their return trip across the border to secure a previously unimaginable future in post-revolutionary Mexico. *Míralo bien*, my grandmother could have insisted, look at it. The wings, flapping rhythmically against the overcast sky. Her voice, a harsh squawk traveling vertical distances. *Eres tú, Cristino, una garza*. It's you, she could have said. Or else, it's us. The heron family. They pause and then, as if taken by surprise, they burst into laughter. It is a deep, hearty laugh, shared in unison—the kind of accord that requires years together, the burying of children, hunger, and trust. The heron glides gracefully, with a bravado they celebrate, and swoops down, landing on the roof of the porch. *Ardea herodias*. *Cristino Heron*, my grandmother Emilia could have said again, still chuckling. Heron, in fact, or garza, for sure, or *Ardea herodias*, why not, like the bird that walks guardedly on the roof of our house and, standing tall, beholding us, wonders.

6: The Point of View of the Dead

Will there be birds flying non-stop over the surpassing disaster? Will they remain airborne, attentive solely to their migratory route, while the dead—human and non-human—freely roam the earth?

In the thought experiment that was *The World Without Us*, a non-fiction book Alan Weisman published in 2007, the earth undergoes a dramatic breakdown once humans disappear: nuclear facilities explode, but nature thrives in New York City and abandoned Korean demilitarized zones. Without the food provided by humans, rats and cockroaches perish. Suburbs become forests in five hundred years and plastics prove to be as long-lasting as we imagined. As damage goes unchecked on this earth without humans, hard structures collapse and new life forms emerge, creating new habitats. The climate mutates. The belonging. While a pervasive desolation encroaches on this world, mourners remain missing. There are no rites of passage. No wake work. No dead. Will they be there, the dead, beholding the ruins of a life that once was? Will the dead be there, conjuring up a future yet unimaginable to us?

The extinction of humans, biological life, and the planet affords anthropologist Elizabeth Povinelli a formula, at once exact and enigmatic, for interpreting the drama of the Anthropocene: Life (life [birth, growth, reproduction] vs. death) vs. Nonlife. Unlike the philosophers of biopolitics, and even of necropolitics, for whom the fundamental conflagration of our world oscillates between the limits established by life and death, Povinelli expands this bipolarity to incorporate "a form of death that starts and ends in Nonlife, which takes us to a time before the life and death of individuals and species, a time of *geos*, of soullessness." Based on anthropological work in Australia, Povinelli offers the desert, the animist, and the virus as "three condensed expressions of the simultaneous grip of the bios and Thanatos, and the unraveling of their relevance." They are, she adds, "the strange dreams one has before fully waking.

They are the ghosts who exist in between two worlds—the world in which the dependent oppositions of life (bios) and death (thanatos) and of Life (bios) and Nonlife (geos) are sensible and dramatic and the world in which these enclosures are no longer relevant, sensible, or practical." Could they be, the dead, right in between these worlds, peeking over the liminal ghosts that populate our strange dreams?

This question of the dead—and not all dead are human—surges around and cloaks an old narrative device when Claire Colebrook ponders the point of view of extinction. Climate change, which is as catastrophic to human life as to the human imaginary, "reveals multiple and incongruent systems for which we don't have a point of view," claims Colebrook as she questions human species' right to life, welcoming an extinction that will extricate humans, for the better, from globalism, extractivism, consumerism, individualism, and hyper-production. The question of the dead becomes one of readability in *Death of the PostHuman*. Once humans perish, inaugurating the timeline of what Povinelli calls soullessness, "the history of the human will remain readable in a quasi-human sense: the earth's strata will be inscribed with the scars of the human capacity to create radical and volatile climatic changes." But, "can we imagine a world without us, *not* as *our* environment or climate? . . . How might we imagine a world without organic perception, without the centered points of views of sensing and world-orienting beings?"

Writers from the Spanish-speaking world have faced the challenge of climate change and extinction in a variety of ways. While the novelists, essayists, and poets discussed below are not known for writing sci-fi or speculative writing per se, they are nonetheless grappling with how to make a point of view beyond human time and perception. Claudia Peña Claros, a Bolivian poet and fiction writer, conjures the impersonal as a point of view for our rural present; Selva Almada, acclaimed Argentinian author of novels and short stories, intertwines and con/fuses the timelines of the living and the dead in the deep time of mourning; and Diego Rodríguez Landeros directly employs the subjunctive.

Claudia Peña Claros has declared that writing, for her, is pure attention. In the opening scene of "Flare," a barefoot man lies under a canopy of trees, struggling to extricate himself from the red mud that slowly but surely overpowers him. He is dying, and language knows it. Flocks of words cohere into paragraphs or disperse into sparse lines as the narrative folds, instead of unfolding, over time. It drifts. It stumbles. "Do trees feel any attachment?" something or someone ponders. A horse and a latch are in the process of forgetting the dying man while everything in the *monte*, which can be translated as "a hill" but more generally as "the open," is affected by this death. Moving effortlessly between the omniscient and limited third-person perspective, the narrative voice does not impersonate but interrogates the landscape with increasingly detailed questions. This millimetric attention, which exposes fiction to its own facticity, builds an impersonal space that rejects political subjectivation. It is the field of the no-person, as linguist Émile Benveniste has argued; or, as Alberto Moreiras put it: "the landscape beyond the I or the we, and thus a landscape toward the third person, toward that that is innominate, toward that that is anonymous." As the dying man laboriously breathes in and breathes out, attempting to give shape to the inconceivable, his hand is slowly becoming not his hand. He is turning into a not-himself before the reader's eyes. Claudia Peña Claros's impersonal perspective does justice to the dying of a man in a monte where the crossing of property lines may bring on a death sentence.

In *No es un río*, Selva Almada's third novel, a fisherman boasts that he knows the monte better than anyone. What surrounds him are not just trees, or his trees, but these trees. "If he looks further down, where the street ends, he can see the river. And, again, it is not a river, it is this river. He has spent more time with it than with anyone else." The fisherman's river is here, by our side; we can feel it flowing under our feet. In this territory, which regional denominations make both opaque and unique, dreams carry "echoes of the future" and the dead leave material traces of themselves where they are buried, fusing the past with the present, and beyond. This is a vibrant territory brimming with secrets, emotional and otherwise, and the novel detects them without necessarily unveiling them. When the fisherman and his nephew meet up with Luisina and Mariela at the local pub, they flirt and rejoice in the women's company, sharing alcohol and cigarettes as the evening grows dark. But as they get ready to leave, the excitement of the encounter still bright in their eyes, a regular warns him in a low voice: "Don't be fooled, my friend, don't you see that they no longer are." The story of the two young women, interspersed throughout a narration that avoids linear development, exposes the multiplicity of timelines that keep the territory alive. The girls are not figments of the imagination, but apparitions—material presences that locals reckon with in an affective deep time all its own.

Mexican author Daniel Rodríguez Landeros has painstakingly explored the water infrastructure of Central Mexico in hybrid works that escape easy characterization. In *Desagüe*, a novel in which fiction and non-fiction interpellate each other, Indra, the main character, embarks on a journey along the Great Drainage Canal of the Valley of Mexico, as he plans on reaching the place where his girlfriend has recently died by suicide: the Tequixquiac tunnel, some forty-seven kilometers of waterworks that, inaugurated in 1900 by President Porfirio Díaz, have violently drained the Valley of Mexico. For Rodríguez Landeros, stories lack clear-cut beginnings and endings, and the hydrological history of Central Mexico is no exception: "to 'disappear' doesn't mean to stop existing; it means to move to an unknown place, to get lost in the intricate alleyways of the world, to languish in its crannies." *Desagüe* labors through many of the crannies of the water alleyways where the dead, never "completely dead," are but "sleeping zombies" waiting for reactivation. Moving through deep time with the uneasy scalpel of the subjunctive in hand, Rodríguez Landeros questions the relationship between fiction and truth: "What if everything were truly just fiction? What if Indra had never arrived that morning, after months of planning, to kilometer zero? . . . What if Porfirio Díaz, as the great strategist he was, hadn't built the Great Drainage Canal, and no one had ever thought to drain the lakes of the Valley of Mexico to build a Western-style city on them? . . . What if the volcanoes hadn't covered, with lava and ash, the natural drainage outlets in this valley that became a basin where water from the mountains accumulated, forming the lakes of Chalco, Xochimilco, Texcoco, Xaltocan and Zumpango? Would everything I am telling now be false?"

7: The LRG Home for Young Women

> Everything is useful to write a house
> as long as you lay the foundations
> of the poem on solid ground.
>
> GERARDO ARANA

If it were a house. If the house stood humble and proud at the end of a cul-de-sac, facing a park where loud, sweaty kids battled hand to hand to sink an orange ball inside a battered hoop. If dogs ran free, mouths agape, competing for an inch of the cement court. If cats. If birds. If we dwelled in that one-story, three-bedroom, one-bathroom house, enveloped by naked red bricks, connected to other houses, as red, as naked, in the public housing compound. If the house lay at the center of the world, and vertical and horizontal lines crossed right through its hearth, leading us up into the sky and down into the underworld. If, as John Berger would have it, we were nearer to our gods and to our dead in that house.

If a hearth.

If we fought within those walls, long tender early battles about the meaning of life. Are we suspended in the sky or thriving in the underworld? Do you know how to give and then how to give up? What is this language piercing our tongues, our arms, our hands? If we loved under the saddle roof, fiercely, wildly, mercilessly.

If I were a sister. If my sister were lost.

If forever began on July 16, 1990, when Liliana Rivera Garza was killed by her ex-boyfriend far from that house and yet always within that house. Which is our center. Which is our hearth. If the femicider remained at large, even to this day. If aghast, if forcibly silenced, if suddenly disarticulated as stringless marionettes, knees pulverized on the floor. If inside a yowl, befuddled. Still. If we left the house, the sky and the underworld of the house, the dream of the house, absconding from the future. Concealing ourselves. If the house, suddenly hollow, vacant and yet inhabited, enveloped by naked red bricks, remained.

Seventh image: It is a stratovolcano, allegedly dead. Nevado de Toluca in Spanish; Xinantécatl in Nahuatl. Long ago, Juan Rulfo took a selfie sitting on its highest summit, the Friar's Peak, some 4670 meters above sea level—an unlit pipe held to his mouth as he looked out over the Lake of the Sun and the Lake of the Moon, separated by a lava dome, and the amplitude of the valley below. Massive explosions during the late Pleistocene, which generated widespread ashfall, and the Holocene, which produced pyroclastic flows, gave the volcano the myriad of eyes with which it returns our gaze, insisting and impassive, undeterred, beholding us wherever we go. Forever within its reach.

If leaked roofs. If rotten hardwood floors. If spiderwebs and termite infestations. If rusted toilets, sinks, faucet levers, shower curtain hooks. If, about to collapse, hard structures were to fall over ruined pieces of furniture, half-sealed cardboard boxes, broken glass. If the grass grew, unyielding, surrounded by wild shrubbery and thorns. If the cedar tree rose, impassive and vertical, wholly unaware.

If time, passing.

If time were to pass or had passed, transforming the climate outside and within.

If in August 2023 a phone call alerted us to a break-in. If street security cameras featured a group of elderly men clad in jeans led by a young woman as they diligently cut the grass, sculpted the cedar, took boxes out and changed the locks, preparing a comeback. If suddenly awoken, fearing the loss of our loss, we drove back to the house at high speed, standing there later, tense as a bowstring, at the end of the cul-de-sac, looking in. If we forcibly opened the doors and, paralyzed by the view, placed ourselves back at the hearth, where vertical and horizontal lines once crossed, leading us up toward our gods and down toward our dead.

If Liliana were there, waiting.

Would she have said that everything began with a line? Draw it, first, on my skin, she would or could have said, right through my sternum and then through the middle of the gap that keeps the lips slightly apart. Redraw the line on the surface of the house, vertical and horizontal at the same time, and then on the table that once held elbows and palms, notebooks and pens; on the coffee cup, chipped; and on the windows that still open to that slender piercing light of late summer evenings in the highest highlands. Redraw it on the surface of the city, through the streets and parks that once welcomed hurried steps. Don't stop there. Look at it, but don't stop there. Redraw it too on the annoyingly blue sky where migratory birds, caught on contrary winds, keep a watch on us, on all of it. Once done, once the task is completed, undraw the lines and the drawing resulting from them, carved on the surface of things. Let's clean.

If we were to write a house. If a house were a communal pact, a collaborative belaboring, a form of direct action that required the time of others, their hands and lungs, their eyes, their hope. If a house were the opposite of war.

If the house were a healing refuge, the place where young women, wounded and free, could find a respite. If the house bore a name, the initials of her name: LRG, and the name embraced them tightly, caring for them and telling their stories.

If you were to come to this house, unannounced.

Fifteenth thesis: In the subjunctive, no one takes anyone's life.

NOTES AND REFERENCES

Introduction
CHRISTINA SHARPE

NOTES

1. Toni Cade Bambara, "What It Is I Think I'm Doing Anyhow," in Janet Sternburg, ed., *The Writer on Her Work* (New York: W.W. Norton, 1980), 153.
2. Dionne Brand in conversation with Christina Sharpe, qtd. in *Nomenclature: New and Collected Poems* (Toronto, ON: McClelland & Stewart, 2022), xxxiv.

A Manifesto for Speculative Relations
JOSEPH M. PIERCE

NOTES

1. For testimony of the Trail of Tears, see Vicki Rozema, ed., *Voices from The Trail of Tears* (Durham, NC: Blair, 2003).
2. This version is somewhat abbreviated and is drawn from the following sources: James Mooney, *Myths of the Cherokee* (1900; New York: Dover, 1995), 258–59, who notes that it was told in nearly identical form by his informants Ayu'ini (Swimmer), Itagunahi (John Ax), and Suyeta; Christopher B. Teuton, *Cherokee Stories of the Turtle Island Liars' Club* (Chapel Hill, NC: University of North Carolina Press, 2012), 234, as told by

Hastings Shade; Christopher B. Teuton, *Cherokee Earth Dwellers: Stories and Teachings of the Natural World* (Seattle: University of Washington Press, 2023), 149–50, which is Teuton's own retelling.

3. For a detailed account of the historical transition and translation of speculation, see Gayle Rogers, *Speculation: A Cultural History from Aristotle to AI* (New York: Columbia University Press, 2021), 9–15.

4. This definition of speculative relations is drawn from, and developed further in, my forthcoming book *Speculative Relations: Indigenous Worlding and Repair*.

5. For an expansive and generous account of being a good relative, see Daniel Heath Justice, *Why Indigenous Literatures Matter* (Waterloo, ON: Wilfrid Laurier University Press, 2018), 72–112. For more on reciprocal recognition, see Leanne Betasamosake Simpson, *As We Have Always Done: Indigenous Freedom through Radical Resistance* (Minneapolis: University of Minnesota Press, 2017), 180–83.

6. See Daniel Heath Justice, *Our Fire Survives the Storm: A Cherokee Literary History* (Minneapolis: University of Minnesota Press, 2006), 19–42.

7. On traditional Cherokee storytelling (teachings), see Teuton, *Cherokee Earth Dwellers*, 32–34.

8. Ashon Crawley, "Otherwise Movements," *The New Inquiry*, January 19, 2015. https://thenewinquiry.com/otherwise-movements/.

9. I use "the Americas" here as a point of departure, though I will question this naming shortly. I am also limiting myself to the Americas, which is to say I am not referring to Africa, Asia, Australia, Aotearoa, or the Pacific Islands, because my experience and my particular understanding of relations is grounded in Turtle Island. I do think much of what I say here is applicable elsewhere, but I am not proposing a universal theory, which would run counter to the tenets of grounded relations.

10. Sylvia Wynter, "Unsettling the Coloniality of Being/Power/Truth/Freedom: Towards the Human, After Man, Its Overrepresentation—An Argument," CR: The New Centennial Review 3, no. 3 (Fall 2003): 257–337.
11. Christina Sharpe, *In the Wake: On Blackness and Being* (Durham, NC: Duke University Press, 2016), 111.
12. Eve Tuck and K. Wayne Yang, "Decolonization Is Not a Metaphor," *Decolonization: Indigeneity, Education & Society* 1, no. 1 (2012): 21.
13. Shawn Wilson, *Research Is Ceremony: Indigenous Research Methods* (Halifax and Winnipeg: Fernwood, 2008), 80.
14. Emil' Keme, "For Abiayala to Live, the Americas Must Die: Toward a Transhemispheric Indigeneity," trans. Adam Coon, *Native American and Indigenous Studies* 5, no. 1 (Spring 2018): 42–68.
15. Teuton, *Cherokee Earth Dwellers*, 21.
16. Again, following Tuck and Yang, "Decolonization Is Not a Metaphor."
17. Patrick Wolfe, "Settler Colonialism and the Elimination of the Native," *Journal of Genocide Research* 8, no. 4 (2006): 387–409.
18. Lorgia García Peña, *The Borders of Dominicanidad: Race, Nation, and Archives of Contradiction* (Durham, NC: Duke University Press, 2016).
19. Daniel Heath Justice, "Notes Toward a Theory of Anomaly," GLQ: *A Journal of Lesbian and Gay Studies* 16, nos. 1–2 (2010): 207–242.
20. This incomplete list was culled from the diary of B.B. Cannon, one of the military officers charged with leading a detachment of 365 Cherokees from Charleston, Tennessee to Indian Territory in October 1837. For more information, see Rozema, *Voices from The Trail of Tears*, 79–92.

A Manifesto for Curation
JANAÍNA OLIVEIRA

NOTES

1. Hans Ulrich Obrist, *The Archipelago Conversations / Hans Ulrich Obrist, Édouard Glissant* (Rio de Janeiro: Cobogó, 2023), 102.
2. Hans Ulrich Obrist, *Caminhos da curadoria* (Rio de Janeiro: Cobogó, 2014), 28.
3. There is an extensive bibliographic production on the subject, including essays, interviews, and academic research, many of which have become books and online publications, or catalogs. Particularly noteworthy are the works of Swiss curator Hans Ulrich Obrist, such as *A Brief History of Curating* (Zurich: JPR Ringier, 2011), and the digital newspaper *Curatography: The Study of Curatorial Culture* (https://curatography.org/), produced by Curating Asia International (CAI).
4. Said Szeemann: "After all, the word curator already contains the concept of care." Harald Szeemann, "Does Art Need Directors?" in *Words of Wisdom: A Curator's Vade Mecum on Contemporary Art*, ed. Carin Kuoni (New York: Independent Curators International, 2001), 67.
5. Kate Fowle, "Who Cares? Understanding the Role of the Curator Today," in *Cautionary Tales: Critical Curating*, ed. Steven Rand and Heather Kuris (New York: apexart, 2010), 26.
6. Olu Oguibe, "The Burden of Curation," *Revista Concinnitas* 1, no. 6 (2019): 6–18, https://www.e-publicacoes.uerj.br/concinnitas/article/view/44475.
7. Thomas Elsaesser, "Curating as Post-production," Curation, cinema, and other ways of showing [electronic resource], org. Gabriel Menotti (Vitória: EDUFES, 2018), 38.
8. Kemi Adeyemi, "Black Women Curators: A Brief Oral History of the Recent Past," in *The Routledge Companion to American Art*

History, ed. Eddie Chambers (New York and London: Routledge, 2020), 429.

9. Gayatri Chakravorty Spivak, *May the Subaltern Speak?* (Belo Horizonte: Editora UFMG, 2010).
10. Ella Shohat and Robert Stam, *Unthinking Eurocentrism* (New York: Routledge, 1994).
11. bell hooks, "Oppositional Gaze," in *Black Looks: Race and Representation* (New York and London: Routledge, 2015), 120.
12. Jota Mombaça, "The Cognitive Plantation," Afterall, https://www.afterall.org/articles/the-cognitive-plantation/.
13. "Encounters for Tomorrow," with Françoise Vergès and Erica Malunguinho, https://www.youtube.com/watch?v=v_xHohZhIsQ.
14. "In this work, *In the Wake: On Blackness and Being*, I want to think 'the wake' as a problem of and for thought. I want to think 'care' as a problem for thought. I want to think care in the wake as a problem for thinking and of and for Black non/being in the world." Christina Sharpe, *In the Wake*: *On Blackness and Being* (Durham, NC: Duke University Press), 12.
15. Girish Shambu, "For a New Cinephilia," *Film Quarterly* 72, no. 3 (2019): 32–34.
16. Rizvana Bradley and Denise Ferreira da Silva, "Four Theses on Aesthetics," *e-flux Journal* #120 (2021).
17. Thomas Elsaesser, "The Ethics of Appropriation: Found Footage between Archive and Internet," *Found Footage Magazine*, issue 1 (2015): 30–37.
18. In October 2023, Venice hosted a second edition of *Loophole of Retreat*, an event organized by Simone Leigh and curated by Rashida Bumray, with Tina Campt and Saidiya Hartman as advisors. *Loophole* was a true portal, a quantum, a choir, a transformative and regenerative experience that will long echo in the seven hundred participants who were there—yes, seven hundred Black women participated in *Loophole of Retreat: Venice*. In many ways, the experience of the speeches heard there

reverberates in this Manifesto. Tina Campt, *Loophole of Retreat: Venice*, https://www.youtube.com/watch?v=91bWInpKlVs.
19. How do you revisit the scene of subjection without replicating the grammar of violence?" asks Hartman in the text "Venus in Two Acts," *Small Axe* 12, no. 2 (2008): 1–14.
20. "What Is Curatography?" https://curatography.org/1-1-en/.
21. Amaranta César, "Living with Cinema: Curation and Programming as an Intervention in History," in *Flow into Cinema: Documentary, Memory, and Action with CachoeiraDoc* [online], ed. A. Cesar, A.R. Marques, F. Pimenta, and L. Costa (Salvador: EDUFBA, 2020), 149.
22. About Opacity, there is a catalog available, published in 2022 and edited by Carol Almeida and Dessane Lopez Cassell, which can be accessed at https://theflaherty.org/2022-opacity-catalog.
23. Christina Sharpe, *In the Wake: On Blackness and Being*, 13.
24. Quoted by Obrist, *Conversations from the Archipelago*, 147.

Manifesto of the As Yet Unlived Thing
PHOEBE BOSWELL

NOTES

1. Lola Olufemi, *Experiments in Imagining Otherwise* (London: Hajar, 2021), 43.
2. Zoé Samudzi (@babywasu), "decolonisation is a horizon, decolonisation has no end," Instagram, October 2023.
3. "Stephen Jenkinson on a Lucid Reckoning," *For the Wild* podcast, ep. 349 (September 20, 2023), https://forthewild.world/listen/stephen-jenkinson-on-a-lucid-reckoning-349.
4. Simone Weil, *Gravity and Grace*, trans. Emma Crawford and Marion von der Ruhr (1947, trans. 1952; London and New York: Routledge Classics, 2004), 33, 39.

Crow Jane Makes a Modest Proposal
SAIDIYA HARTMAN

NOTES
1. Jonathan Swift, A Modest Proposal (1729).
2. W.E.B. Du Bois, *Black Reconstruction* (1935).
3. Toni Morrison, *Playing in the Dark: Whiteness and the Literary Imagination* (New York: Vintage, 1992), xi.
4. Zakkiyah Iman Jackson, *Becoming Human: Matter and Meaning in an Antiblack World* (New York: New York University Press, 2020).

Subjunctive: A Manifesto about Language, Territory, and the Yet to Come
CRISTINA RIVERA GARZA

REFERENCES
1. My heartfelt thanks to Cheyla Samuelson, Robin Myers, and Sarah Booker for meticulously reading and generously commenting on this draft.
2. On page 120, references to the participation of my paternal and maternal grandparents in the making of a border of cotton between Texas and Tamaulipas come from *Autobiografía del algodón* (New York: Penguin Random House, 2020).
3. On page 121, the reference to the angel of history comes from Walter Benjamin's "Theses on the Philosophy of History" (1940).
4. On page 123, Ashley M. Jones's poem is called "Summer Vacation in the Subjunctive," published in *REPARATIONS NOW!* (Spartanburg, SC: Hub City Press, 2021).
5. On pages 125 and 145, references to Claire Colebrook, *Death of the PostHuman: Essays on Extinction, Vol. 1* (London: Open Humanities Press, 2014).

6. On page 125, José Revueltas discussed his concepts of "ubicación" and "pertenencia" in the essay "The Writer and the Land," included in *El luto humano (Obras Completas de José Revueltas no. 2)*, (Mexico City: Era, 1980).
7. On page 126, the book by Bradford Burns is *The Poverty of Progress: Latin America in the Nineteenth Century* (Berkeley: University of California Press, 1983).
8. On page 127, reference to Aymara alternative mapping of time is based on Silvia Rivera Cusicanqui, *Sociología de la imagen: Miradas chi'ixi desde la historia andina* (Buenos Aires: Tinta Limón, 2015).
9. On page 128, see Joanna Zylinska, *The End of Man: A Feminist Counterapocalypse* (Minneapolis, MN: University of Minnesota Press, 2018).
10. On page 129, see Floriberto Díaz, *Escrito: Comunalidad, e nergía viva del pensamiento mixe,* ed. Sofía Robles Hernández and Rafael Cardoso Jiménez (Mexico City: Libros UNAM, 2007), a book yet to be translated into English. Additional readings about communality include Jaime Martínez Luna, *Eso que llaman comunalidad* (Mexico City: Conaculta, 2010); Gladys Tzul Tzul, *Sistemas de gobierno comunal indígena* (Mexico City: Libertad bajo palabra, 2016).
11. On page 129, see Anna Tsing, *The Mushroom at the End of the World: On the Possibility of Life in Capitalist Ruins* (Princeton, NJ: Princeton University Press, 2015).
12. On page 134, reference to James Scott, *Against the Grain: A Deep History of the Earliest States* (New Haven, CT: Yale University Press, 2017).
13. On page 135, the phrase by José Salazar Ylarregui comes from *Datos de los trabajos astronómicos y topográficos por la Comisión de Límites Mexicana* (Mexico City: Imprenta de Juan Navarro, 1850).
14. On page 137, see Georges Didi-Huberman, *Images In Spite of All: Four Photographs of Auschwitz* (Chicago, IL: University of Chicago Press, 2012).

15. On page 138, the piece by Laure Prouvost can be found at https://circa.art/press/press-release-laure-provoust-no-more-front-tears/.
16. On pages 138 and 139, the quotations from Georges Perec are from his book *Ellis Island*, trans. Harry Matthews (New York: New Directions, 2021).
17. On page 140, see Gloria Anzaldúa, *Borderlands/La Frontera: The New Mestiza* (San Francisco, CA: Aunt Lute Books, 1987).
18. On page 142, essays by Yásnaya Elena Aguilar have been compiled in *Ää: Manifiestos sobre la diversidad lingüística* (Mexico City: Almadía, 2020). Some of the references quoted here come from in-depth interviews published by the Spain-based newspaper *El país*, where Aguilar maintains a monthly column, and the University of Chile: https://uchile.cl/noticias/178190/yasnaya-aguilar-y-la-lengua-como-pilar-de-la-autonomia-de-los-pueblos. Also by this author: *Inventar lo posible: Manifiestos mexicanos contemporáneos* (2017), *Un nosotrxs sin estado* (2018).
19. On page 143, the reference is to Don Mee Choi, *Translation Is a Mode = Translation Is an Anti-neocolonial Mode* (New York: Ugly Duckling Presse, 2020).
20. On page 144, see Alan Weisman, *The World Without Us* (London: Picador, 2008).
21. On page 144, see Elizabeth Povinelli, *Geontologies: A Requiem to Late Liberalism* (Durham, NC: Duke University Press, 2016).
22. On page 146, see Claudia Peña Claros, *Los árboles* (La Paz: El Cuervo, 2019). Translations by the author.
23. On page 147, see Selva Almada, *No es un río* (New York: Penguin Random House, 2020). Translations by the author.
24. On page 147, see Diego Rodríguez Landeros, *Desagüe* (Mexico City: FCE, 2019). Translations by the author. For an excerpt from *Desagüe* translated into English by Louis Sanger, see https://latinamericanliteraturetoday.org/2023/06/an-excerpt-from-desague/.

ABOUT THE ALCHEMISTS

PHOEBE BOSWELL (UK/Kenya) explores the liminal space between our collective histories and imagined futures; how we see ourselves and each other, and, consequently, how we free ourselves, or imagine freedom. Her figurative, interdisciplinary practice moves intuitively between drawing, painting, video, sonics, interactivity, chirality, and writing. Her work is held in collections including the British Museum, LACMA, RISD, the BFI's National Archive, and the UK Government Art Collection. She was the Bridget Riley Drawing Fellow at the British School at Rome in 2019, received the Paul Hamlyn Award for Artists in 2019, the Lumière Award from the Royal Photographic Society in 2021, and was Whitechapel Gallery's 2022 writer-in-residence. She has presented her writing at Tate Britain, the Victoria & Albert Museum, the Ford Foundation, and *Loophole of Retreat: Venice*, and has had institutional solos at Autograph ABP, New Art Exchange, and Göteborgs Konsthall. Boswell was born in Nairobi and lives and works in London.

SAIDIYA HARTMAN (US) is the author of *Wayward Lives, Beautiful Experiments: Intimate Histories of Social Upheaval* (2019), *Lose Your Mother: A Journey Along the Atlantic Slave Route* (2006), and *Scenes of Subjection: Terror, Slavery, and Self-Making in Nineteenth-Century America* (1997). A MacArthur Genius Fellow, she has been a Guggenheim Fellow, Cullman Fellow, and Fulbright Scholar. She is a University Professor at Columbia University and is in the Department of English and Comparative Literature. In addition to her books, she has published articles in journals such as *South Atlantic Quarterly, Brick, Small Axe, Callaloo, The New Yorker,* and *The Paris Review.*

JANAÍNA OLIVEIRA (Brazil) is a film scholar and independent curator. Professor at the Federal Institute of Rio de Janeiro (IFRJ) and consultant for JustFilms/Ford Foundation, Oliveira has a Ph.D. in History and was a Fulbright Visiting Scholar at the Center for African Studies at Howard University. Since 2009, she has researched and made film programs mainly focusing on Black and African Cinemas. She has also worked as a consultant, juror, and panelist in several film festivals and institutions in Brazil and abroad. In 2019, she programmed the "Soul in the Eye: Zózimo Bulbul legacies and the Contemporary Black Brazilian Cinema" series at the International Film Festival Rotterdam, and also worked as an advisor for African and Black diaspora films for the Locarno Film Festival (2019-2020). She is the founder of the Black Cinema Itinerant Forum (FICINE), and was the Flaherty Film Seminar (New York) programmer for 2021 and of Zózimo Bulbul Black Film Festival (Rio de Janeiro) from 2017 to 2021.

ABOUT THE ALCHEMISTS

JOSEPH M. PIERCE (Cherokee Nation) is Associate Professor in the Department of Hispanic Languages and Literature at Stony Brook University. His research focuses on the intersections of kinship, gender, sexuality, and race in Latin America, 19th century literature and culture, queer studies, Indigenous studies, and hemispheric approaches to citizenship and belonging. He is the author of *Argentine Intimacies: Queer Kinship in an Age of Splendor, 1890-1910* (2019) and co-editor of *Políticas del Amor: Derechos Sexuales y Escrituras Disidentes en el Cono Sur* (2018), as well as the 2021 special issue of *GLQ*, "Queer/Cuir Américas: Translation, Decoloniality, and the Incommensurable." His work has been published recently in *Revista Hispánica Moderna, Critical Ethnic Studies, Latin American Research Review*, and has also been featured in *Indian Country Today*. Along with S.J. Norman (Koori of Wiradjuri descent) he is co-curator of the performance series *Knowledge of Wounds*.

CRISTINA RIVERA GARZA (US/Mexico) is the author of six novels, four collections of short stories, five collections of poetry, and four nonfiction books. The recipient of the Roger Caillois Award for Latin American Literature (Paris, 2013), as well as the Anna Seghers Prize (Berlin, 2005), she is the only author who has won the International Sor Juana Inés de la Cruz Prize twice. She is Distinguished Professor in Hispanic Studies and Director of the Ph.D. in Creative Writing in Spanish at the University of Houston. Rivera Garza is the recipient of a 2020 MacArthur Fellowship; her book, *Grieving*, was a finalist for the 2020 National Book Critics Circle Award for Criticism, and *Liliana's Invincible Summer: A Sister's Search for Justice* was a finalist for the 2023 National Book Award and won the 2024 Pulitzer Prize in Memoir. Born in Mexico in 1964, she has lived in the United States since 1989.

ACKNOWLEDGEMENTS

For their support, intellectual and material, without which the Lecture could not have happened, we thank the following people, groups, and organizations:

Andrea Davis for her support and collaboration. We are grateful for the work of Jan Anderson, Research Assistant and Ph.D. Candidate in Humanities at York University, whose organizational skills are unparalleled.

The Office of the President of York University, JJ McMurtry and the Office of the Dean of the Faculty of Liberal Arts and Professional Studies. Ravi de Costa, Associate Dean, Research and Graduate Studies in the Faculty of Liberal Arts & Professional Studies.

The Canada Research Chair in Black Studies in the Humanities at York University; the Faculty of Liberal Arts & Professional Studies; the Department of Humanities; the Graduate Program in Humanities; the Black Canadian Studies Certificate; Social and Political Thought; the LA&PS Anti-Black Racism Research Initiatives Fund; the Department of English; the Faculty of Education; Robarts Centre for Canadian Studies; Eve Haque and the York Research Chair in Linguistic

ACKNOWLEDGEMENTS

Diversity & Community Vitality; Carl James and the Jean Augustine Chair in Education, Community and Diaspora; Natalie Diaz and the Center for Imagination in the Borderlands, Arizona State University; Rinaldo Walcott and the Carl V. Granger Chair in Africana and American Studies, University of Buffalo; Canisia Lubrin and the School of English and Theatre Studies, University of Guelph; David Chariandy and the Department of English, University of Toronto; and Dionne Brand, Editorial Director at Alchemy by Knopf Canada.

Thank you to the Communications and Publicity people at York University: Nathalia Wittingham, Nazrin Vakilova, Sasha Smith, Victoria Stacey, Nicole Glassman, Sanja Begic, Krishika Gupta, Anam Raheel, and Sissi Song. Thanks to Penguin Random House Canada/Knopf Canada, including CEO Kristin Cochrane, whose enthusiastic response to this initiative has made the publication process possible; Adrienne Tang and Cat Ryoo for their attention to international rights; Jennifer Griffiths for her striking design of the cover and interior, alongside Susan Burns and Christie Hanson for their care with the physical production of the book; Ashley Dunn for her marketing vision for the series and Cameron Waller for publicity; and the small, passionate Alchemy team for their care in shepherding the book through all its stages: Dionne Brand, Editorial Director of Alchemy; Martha Kanya-Forstner, Publisher of Knopf Canada; Lynn Henry, Publishing Director of Alchemy; and Hilary Lo, Assistant Editor at Knopf Canada and Alchemy.

Above all, we wish to thank again the Lecturers for all the extraordinary ways in which they thought together, on stage and in the pages of this book.